Praise for

Worrying: A Literary and Cultural History

"Francis O'Gorman offers a witty, philosophical meditation on the meaning of worry, where it comes from and how it came to be our constant companion ... Although the visual arts and music can provide temporary distraction for the worrier, we need words—fragile, unstable words—to express it. Thankfully O'Gorman has given us some more."
—Liz Hoggard, *The Independent*

"In his highly anxious but very valuable new book, Francis O'Gorman seeks to pin down worry as an idea and to record the stories we tell ourselves about it; he sets worrying in both its recent and its deeper cultural history, and he also contemplates the various ways writers and artists have dealt with worry as a category of experience ... *Worrying* also fits into the tradition of breaking down myths and tropes into discrete units, a bit like Mircea Eliade's *Myth and Reality* or C. S. Lewis's *Studies in Words*. We care about these books because we need stories about the cultural past so that we might have a sense of ourselves in time. The real value of O'Gorman's book lies, I think, in the way it flags the politics of the stories we tell ourselves."
—Josephine Livingstone, *New Republic*

"[An] affectionate tribute to low-level fretting ... Mr O'Gorman is a pleasant and good-humored guide, and his candid, self-effacing style helps mitigate any boredom. If there is a message, it addresses the ever-expanding cottage industry around happiness and wellbeing ... Mr O'Gorman's celebration of the wonderful eccentricity of human nature is both refreshing and necessary."
—*The Economist*

"The best parts of this book, as you would hope from a literary critic, are the textual readings. O'Gorman doesn't just provide illuminating discussions of worry literature ... He also reads worry per se as a literary trope, a 'comedy of mental manners' in which its victims are like stage characters trapped in their humors, always enacting the same scenes and parroting the same catchphrases. He is often dryly funny himself ... While it failed to assuage any of my worries, this winning little book still made me root for and, yes, worry a little for its author. I hope this review stops him fretting for a bit, at least until the next worry arrives."
—Joe Moran, *The Guardian*

"An engagingly personal quest to find out 'what [worry] means, both for good and bad' ... [S]ome of the most striking parts of this book are those in which [O'Gorman] shares some illuminating intuition about worry—that it can be 'a species of self-indulgence, a way of extending ego into a conversation, or of somehow confirming selfness in the head'; or that worriers might, deep down, think too highly of themselves, believe that they are 'too good to err and certainly too good to admit errors or apologize for them.'"

—Catherine Morris, *Times Literary Supplement*

"It is worth reading for many reasons, but surely because it treats worrying as a complex issue, that is to say, as a feeling that might have a lot of good stuff to be said about it. *Worrying* works because it's not all doom and gloom, it avoids self-pity, and manages to have both an intellectual and personal discussion of an emotional issue from various and surprising angles."

—Charlie Pullen, *The Bookbag*

"It is 4.06 am. Francis O'Gorman is in bed. His partner and three cats lie fast asleep beside him. But he is awake, worrying. So begins this subtle, exploratory, completely original book."

—John Carey, *The Sunday Times*

"[An] intelligent and probing study."

—James Williams, *The Tablet*

"In some enjoyably subversive pages, [O'Gorman] unpicks a few of modernity's best-loved fairy tales."

—Dan Hitchens, *The Spectator*

"Worrying is not a self-help book. In fact, it frequently pokes holes in that genre. Nor is the book spiritual in any sense. As the book's subtitle suggests, this is a literary and cultural history, as well as a personal one (O'Gorman is a self-confessed worrier). The book is an exercise in worrying about worry."

—Karen Swallow Prior, *Christianity Today*

"Keeping us up with his sleepless stresses—did I forget to lock the door downstairs?—Francis O'Gorman comes to think that such anxieties, rather than being just a niggling malfunction, might also represent a constructive aspect of the human condition. What's the use of worrying?"

—Rachel Bowlby, Professor of Comparative Literature, Princeton University, USA, and author of *A Child of One's Own: Parental Stories*

Francis O'Gorman, from English, Irish, and Hungarian families, was born in 1967 and educated as C. S. Deneke Organ Scholar of Lady Margaret Hall, Oxford, where he took a double first and a doctorate in English literature. He is the author or editor of 23 books, mostly on English literature, and of essays on literature, music, and the condition of the modern English university. His *Worrying: A Literary and Cultural History* (Bloomsbury, 2015), described by John Carey as "subtle, exploratory, completely original," was a *Guardian* "Book of the Week," a *Sunday Times* "Must Read," and one of Bookbag's "History Books of the Year, 2015." For a decade, Francis O'Gorman held a chair in the School of English at the University of Leeds; he is now Saintsbury Professor of English Literature at the University of Edinburgh. When not working, he likes playing the organ, walking Arthur's Seat, or sitting in a bar.

Forgetfulness

Making the Modern
Culture of Amnesia

Francis O'Gorman

Bloomsbury Academic
An imprint of Bloomsbury Publishing Inc

B L O O M S B U R Y
NEW YORK · LONDON · OXFORD · NEW DELHI · SYDNEY

Bloomsbury Academic
An imprint of Bloomsbury Publishing Inc

1385 Broadway
New York
NY 10018
USA

50 Bedford Square
London
WC1B 3DP
UK

www.bloomsbury.com

**BLOOMSBURY and the Diana logo are trademarks of Bloomsbury
Publishing Plc**

First published 2017

Library of Congress Cataloging-in-Publication Data
A catalog record for this book is available from the Library of Congress.

ISBN: HB: 978-1-5013-2469-7
ePub: 978-1-5013-2470-3
ePDF: 978-1-5013-2471-0

Cover design: Jason Anscomb/rawshock design
Photo credit: Francis O'Gorman

Typeset by Newgen Knowledge Works Pvt Ltd., Chennai, India
Printed and bound in the United States of America

To find out more about our authors and books visit www.bloomsbury.com. Here
you will find extracts, author interviews, details of forthcoming events, and the
option to sign up for our newsletters.

Today the air is clear of everything.
It has no knowledge except of nothingness
And it flows over us without meaning,
As if none of us had ever been here before
And are not now: in this shallow spectacle,
This invisible activity, this sense.

"A Clear Day and No Memories," Wallace Stevens (1879–1955)
Opus Posthumous ([1957] 1989)

"We must not think we have an easy task when we have a difficult task, or that we are living in a natural state when we are really living in an artificial one."

Walter Bagehot, *Lombard Street: A Description of the Money Market* (1910)

Photograph by Francis O'Gorman, 2016

Contents

Introduction 1

1   Cultures of memory 17

2   The making of modern forgetting 33

3   Contemporary cultures of amnesia 65

4   Forgetfulness in contemporary cultural narratives 99

5   Learning pasts 123

6   The problems of forgetting national and local
    histories 145

Acknowledgments 171
References 173
Index 183

Introduction

"Here is a good deal of room for mistake and prodigality before you come to the edge of ruin."

EDMUND BURKE

Observations on a Late Publication, intituled
"The Present State of the Nation" (1769)

How was I going to begin? What was I planning to say?
I can't remember.
I should have written it down when it first occurred to me.
Oh dear.

* * *

The experience of forgetting is routine. We have a choice of words and phrases for regular, common-or-garden forgetting in English in case we become bored with the familiarity of "I've forgotten." The choice includes: "I can't recall," "it's gone out of my head," "I've lost my train of thought," "it's slipped my mind," "it's on the tip of my tongue," "it'll come back to me," "it's gone."

Ordinary forgetting can be a source of embarrassment and frustration—as well as mystery. I sometimes forget what a student has just said to me in a seminar and I mean, literally, *just said to me*. I stare blankly for a moment. I feel a mild physical sense of panic because my response has been taken away.

There are worse torments. Some of those are experienced by people who are about to speak in public—to a business meeting, a lecture room, a live TV or radio audience. The anxiety is that, at some point, there will be nothing more to say because the speaker's mind will, as we phrase it in another one of those synonymous expressions, have "gone blank." This is familiar, too. So much so that there is professional advice on YouTube about how to handle temporary loss of words in public: search "Uh oh, I have forgotten what I was going to say." If the ordinary human brain has an extraordinary capacity to recall, it has also a disturbing capacity to let us down.

"Sorry … er …"

Memory, as a word in English, probably has its roots in the Latin *memoria*. That simply means "mindful" or "remembering." But the Latin has an uncomfortable Attic shadow just as the triumph of Rome is always conscious of the story of Greece that it replaces. Μέρμερος (*mermeros*), a second declension noun, means "causing anxiety," "baneful," "woeful," "mischievous." It is the etiolated Athenian sister of Rome's recollection. *Mermeros*, for us, is a faint etymological reminder that aspiring to remember can be trouble.

Modern memory science advises its audiences that much of what we remember is, however, predicated on forgetting. We think we are remembering but actually we are selecting. Take the idea of a "first memory." Sigmund Freud (1856–1939) alerts his readers to the fact that this "first memory" is likely nothing of the sort—that the brain has stored a huge amount of previous experience but that we have chosen to remember what we name the "first" memory because it encodes an important meaning about our lives.

I remember, in our house in the Shropshire countryside, feeding our domestic chickens with earthworms through wire netting. I was surprised that their beaks didn't hurt when they accidentally pecked at my fingers. Dimly I didn't like the fact that I was feeding living creatures to other living creatures. Later, or perhaps before, I remember inadvertently stepping on a grass-snake—it was unharmed—when I thought there was only a roadside verge. I can't say which of these came first.

I wonder if either reveals anything deep. Certainly, they both clinch—now I think about it—my understanding that other animals share this planet and that I must try not to harm them. I've been a vegetarian for more than a quarter of a century. Perhaps these memories capture, too, my fundamental expectation that I am going to be injured or accidentally cause pain; that I am endangered or somehow in the wrong simply for doing what I do. Maybe I recall those hens because they surprised me, against my habitual emotional logic, because they *didn't* hurt. It could be that I recollect that snake because, in conformity to my internal logic, I had no intention of causing distress but accidentally did.

"First memories," as Freud suggests, may involve a good deal of strategic, tactical, or deliberate (if subconscious) forgetting. They are the product, perhaps, of choosing as well as remembering. And they may not be a product of memory at all. It is possible—though I don't *think* so—that mine are inventions.

We understand, from contemporary memory science, that recollections change. We know science comprehends that "memory" is not static but dynamic. Modern readers realize, too, as Charles Fernyhough's *Pieces of Light: How the New Science of Memory Illuminates the Stories We Tell about Our Pasts* (2012) explains, that what an individual believes about an event is mobile. What we think we remember of something is changeful. For such science, the important matter to understand is an altering mental relationship with a fact—or an apparent fact—not the fact itself as a single unmediated and empirically stable occasion.

This book keeps an eye on personal memory in all its chameleon changefulness. But personal histories are not my principal topic, however much they inform the shape of this investigation. *Forgetfulness: Making the Modern Culture of Amnesia* isn't primarily about an individual forgetting so much as about groups, communities, and societies failing to remember; about how to relate the quotidian experience of personal memory loss to a wider atmosphere of mental blankness. My primary focus is on collective memories: on how a human being in the liberal West relates to communal rather than private yesterdays, to pasts that are not merely ours but others'.

Forgetfulness does not assume—taking a lesson from modern memory science—that acts of remembering, cultural or personal, are simple. "To remember" is an active verb and so is "to forget." This book does not, either, propose uncritical or merely sentimental thinking about collective history, or accept as a matter of conviction that "things were always better in the past." The aim of my book—to summarize roughly—is to explore why we have ceased to consider, save for that which can be turned into a profit or an exam, that the past has much meaning, pleasure, or importance at all.

We forget of necessity, through bodily weakness, through the destruction of records, and because of the uncertain meaning of survivals. Sometimes we try actively: we knowingly *choose* to forget— and are not wrong to do so. On occasions, we would *like* to forget, but can't. Shakespeare's Juliet wishes earnestly that she could lose from mind the fact that Romeo has been banished after Tybalt's death. "I would forget it fain," she says, "But, O, it presses to my memory, | Like damned guilty deeds to sinners' minds" (Act 3, Sc.2, ll. 109–11). That might be Macbeth speaking, too. But it is not personal sorrow only that benefits from a less than perfect memory. Compromise and peace often require, for nations as well as for individuals, an ability to overlook—as David Rieff's *In Praise of Forgetting: Historical Memory and Its Ironies* (2016) most recently describes. "Truth and reconciliation" are not synonyms. Sometimes a nation must forget—or at least officially "move on from"—what another did to it in order to survive. Sometimes an individual must obliterate from his or her mind, or pretend to, what the manager said in the photocopying room in order to keep going.

But my book isn't a study of that kind of sensible forgetting either. Its first assumption is that there is a relationship between, on the one side, human pleasure, wisdom, identity, and security, and, on the other, what we know of the best and most interesting of the past. And my book's second assumption is that we have largely failed to remember this. For the contemporary West, what is past, as I contend here, has become like the lost city of Atlantis. We do not know where it is and we are not sure it ever existed. In turn, *Forgetfulness* is about waves of amnesia that are neither a product of weak memories nor rational decisions to move beyond quarrels but of societal and economic determinations, of commercial choices and secular obligations, of the fixed regimes of acceptable thinking about time in advanced capitalism. *Forgetfulness* concerns the disappearance of pasts that we have forced on ourselves and on others.

I am looking for where history has gone—and how it has come to disappear. This book narrates a phenomenon, which commences in earnest in the nineteenth century, and explores its implications. This Copernican change is the almost completely successful attempt by modernity—I define what I mean by this in Chapter 2—to focus human minds on the future, or at least on the "described-as-future." A result of this orientation to unknown times ahead is an erasure of the past: a more or less successful program to downgrade history and render care about it a sign of weakness, a matter of sentiment or opinion only, a badge that proclaims one's unfitness for membership of the contemporary world's advanced, and supposedly advancing, citizenry. There are important precursors to this condition of mind prior to the nineteenth century's entrancement with tomorrow. But the real development of our enthrallment with forgetfulness, and the elongated romance with what is to come, properly commences in the period of electricity, telegraphy, and telephones. The twenty-first century is the inheritor of the nineteenth. In the United Kingdom, even the sewers are theirs. And the West also repeats, as it has intensified, that century's gluey adhesion to what lies ahead.

I describe the emergence of a forgetfulness culture, the state of mind brilliantly upturned by Samuel Beckett in *Endgame* (*Fin de partie*, 1957): "CLOV: Do you believe in the life to come? HAMM: Mine was always that." But then I wonder what we can do about it. This is a book in defense of active and analytical remembering; in taking the trouble to think about achievement rather than simply about promise. It encourages an intellectual willingness to resist modernity's dismissal, or mere monetization, of the past and to think independently about what we could gain from memory. Capitalist modernity's breathless desire is to forget. It is to draw a veil over histories, cultural narratives from the past, artifacts and achievements bequeathed to us by predecessors, and identities shaped by time, in preference for unknown material and ideological prosperities allegedly to come. My book is a meditation on what we have done to foster this dedication to forgetfulness, a set of reflections on our cultural disenfranchisement and its attendant frustrations.

Forgetfulness explores how and why we have come to assume that we must live without (most) histories—histories that are complex and rich, strange and contradictory, vital and difficult, painful as well as instructive, pleasurable as well as sad. It is a book about why we prefer—as Freud made clear—history as trauma rather than as gain. My book examines why the literature, music, and art of the past has become accessible to the young almost entirely as subjects for school or university tests and of little more advanced use, delight, profitable confusion, or sense beyond that. *Forgetfulness* explores why thinking seriously about historical achievements has become the domain of a few, about whom modernity is generally suspicious. The loss of history is measured in the anorexic deterioration of Western taste (though I admit that such deterioration has been lamented since anyone had a notion of taste at all) and its understanding of aesthetic and intellectual achievement. But this loss is also measured in the multiple forms of modern rootlessness—in loneliness, dislocation, sorrow, and conceptual as well as sometimes literal homelessness. Faced with forgotten ideas and forgotten people, and urged only to strive for future achievement seemingly promised in a plan, Western modernity is the hectic location of the lost who only imagine they know where they are going. "We have," as the Australian poet Peter Porter (1929–2010) expressed it, "our loneliness | And our regret with which to build an eschatology." We can look to what is to come only from a position of absence and lack.

Forgetfulness assesses the intellectual, cultural, and psychic wounds inflicted by what I claim to be the modern world's continual winding-down of the portcullis on history. The book's principal intention is to understand how and why this has come about. And my purpose is also, at the level of aesthetics—including writing, the visual arts, and architecture—to document some modest but intellectually consequential resistance to this loss, from the nineteenth century to the present day. The rebels in my book—such rebellion as is possible in the conformist regimes of bureaucratic modernity—include those entranced by forgotten things or at least by the emotional drama of things being forgotten. The rebels here are enthralled by the protests that lie in discerning surviving remains or imagining them. These resistant figures, in different ways, understand and put into language a little of the compound fracture modernity has wrought on our relationship with time.

Modernity's attachment to an idea of future material and ideological reward comes into sharpest focus with a comparison. So my first chapter opens with an emblem: with a visit to the ruins of ancient Mycenaean civilization that are representative of what I (too) boldly generalize as the "memory cultures" of the ancient Mediterranean. My point is not to hold this discussion up as a comprehensive analysis of a forerunner of ancient Greece. Nor do I crudely raise Mycenae into some kind of ancient ideal to which we should all aspire. But thinking about the principal outlines of Mycenae clarifies, however inexactly, structural differences between there and here, between then and now, which are useful to me. A memory culture's relationship with time is one in which the past is central: the primary location of meaning and the ground of duty, respect, and law. In the classical conception of the *polis*— the city as the foundation of citizenship—the ancient peoples of the Mediterranean formalized their understanding of what history meant. And thereby that remote, sunny world codified human identities as defined within, and belonging to, a whole. Analyzing this model of citizenship makes it easy to perceive, and measure, the alternative conceptual architecture of today.

Early Christianity—I take St. Augustine of Hippo (354–430) as representative—played a role in refocusing minds away from the ancient world's engagement with the past toward a concentration on a heavenly future. The alteration in the mental direction of Europe, in the West's relationship with chronology more generally, had commenced. But secular modernity, born of technological, cultural, and economic change in recent times, refocused more thoroughly those minds on a future that was not heavenly but terrestrial. My second chapter, in turn, narrates the rise of this absorption with the future in nineteenth-century intellectual, political, literary, and material history.

The French Revolution, from 1789, is a decisive indication of the political forces that helped mutate modern conceptions of chronology. The events that followed from the storming of the prison of the Bastille on July 14, 1789, luminously, and violently, disclosed how the past, in the form of *l'ancien régime*, could be dismantled by human intervention. Orientating minds toward what could be altered rather than retained, the implications of the Revolution were expanded by subsequent developments in material history and capitalist practice to which we are now *asservi*. The symptomatic document of post-Revolutionary Europe's new relationship with the future is the railway timetable, the text that tells its reader what is (probably) to come. Chapter 2 explores the complex manifestations of the nineteenth century's enchantment with the next, from the serial publishing of fiction (the novel is the exemplary literary form of the century and intimately related to the age's reorientation to the pleasures of suspense) to the operation of the stock exchange and the communication systems that followed in the wake of the railways. This chapter also, in the last portion, creates space to examine a cluster of nineteenth-century cultural critics and writers who mourned the passing of the past. These are men and women who offered a sequence of visual practices and created a range of narratives that involved, or fantasized, identities still in touch with history or wanting to be.

Chapter 3 continues my story to the present day by evaluating what can only be called the contemporary West's intoxication with the promise of the future. The French Revolution taught its champions the benefits of rejecting the past—as the Cromwellians had earlier in the history of Great Britain, and the Protestants more generally had in continental Europe and North America. But the modern world can think of little else. Continuing with material histories in the first instance, this chapter assesses what the experience of contemporary communication, transport, and urban geography does to our day-to-day understanding of time and memory. The discussion moves, then, to consider other documents and procedures of modern labor, culminating in an investigation of modern business's passion for what has yet to occur, symptomatically clinched in the employee's "personal development plan." This chapter compares modernity's bewitchment with the next—and the concomitant requirement to forget—with ideas from psychoanalysis, contrasting, for instance, that bewitchment with the most familiar of Western humanity's narratives of future gain: those of falling in love. The second half of my chapter places more investigative pressure on what modernity actually means by "the future," suggesting that, despite appearances, the future to which our minds are so comprehensively directed is often chimerical. I survey false futures—including ones that are apparently obtained simply by saying that they have been obtained—and explore how difficult it is to recognize what is actually new without a memory. I note, too, that modernity's futures are always anyway replaced by new ones as if reaching an end-point is by definition a disappointing experience: plans follow plans. Modernity, I conclude, encourages faith in a prospect of time to come that never comes, or which we cannot recognize when it does.

So where, Chapter 4 inquires, does our conscience go, our ethical assessment of what is happening? Encouraged to privilege the unknown pledge of tomorrow, we are detached from an understanding that yesterday has much worthwhile meaning. "Innovation," "opportunity," the "entrepreneur," and "growth" are the talismanic charms of advanced capitalism's faith in the next. And they help us neglect the achievements of history with all the consequent implications of that bereavement for complex individual and collective identities sustained through time. But in some highly visible Western narratives, which are of persistent contemporary interest, encrypted ideas about what is happening are, I think, dimly present. Chapter 4 explores, at first, the subtexts of the modern fascination with dementia, stroke recovery, and autism. Here is an Aristotelian fascination of pity and fear. Narratives that arise from these medical topics speak obviously to the commonness of the medical or cognitive conditions they describe. But in different ways these narratives also present coded images not only of individual human beings in difficulty but of Western modernity as a whole in trouble.

I examine stroke-recovery narratives, for instance, as oblique tales of how to return to memory. The longing to restore the self by restoring the self's past—like the longing for a cure for dementia—figures personal hopes but also cultural desires to be in touch with histories once again. In the modern preoccupation with cognitive disorders, modernity processes a complicated version of itself too: one where there appears to be little comprehension of the past except as something that is a symptom of a problem of knowing. Chapter 4 concludes by musing on what revelation, what self-understanding, is to be disinterred from a number of therapeutic practices in mental health care in addition to those prominent narratives from modern medicine and psychology. My final subject is the commitment of psychoanalysis and Cognitive Behavioral Therapy to the past as a scene of misfortune. These are practices that confirm an assumption of the modern world, but they also provide an opportunity, for those able to attend, to hear that assumption articulated.

Chapter 5 thinks not about the cultural conscience but a lack of it. Its subject is what has happened to the past among those who might, on first appearance, have been expected to celebrate its achievements and extend our knowledge of it. The past among the intellectuals and policy advisors who shape educational curricula and assessment regimes appears to have been turned into something merely subjective and amateurish. That is where such pasts are not regarded only as a topic for criticism and reproach. These forces add to the cultural preference for forgetting by providing those educated within such terms with a set of further apparent reasons to neglect or negate history. I examine two main reasons for this decay in care (though there are many others). The first is the influence of poststructuralism in leaving behind a conviction that the past has no distinctive or definite meaning. The second is the contemporary preference among liberal intellectuals for a new kind of Whig history: one where the past is to be surveyed primarily to expose its failings and a slow struggle through time toward the present's own values and achievements.

Chapter 5 assesses the unintended but nonetheless real dissolution of a serious care for the achievements of the past or a willingness to extend and celebrate them among current ideas about what intellectual development is supposed to look like. The chapter's subjects are exam papers, popular conceptions of an education in the arts and humanities, and the difficulties of understanding history in a culture that has privileged immediate gratification and unstrenuous rewards that are, often enough, envisaged as someone else's responsibility to provide. History's most stimulating and demanding attainments have only a limited chance of being perceived in a political culture that has made its highest educational ambition "satisfaction." In analyzing the curious disinclination of the custodians of historical achievements to defend them, the chapter turns to ancient Greece to find a model, in Socrates, of a more questioning approach to the intellectual problems involved in history's dissolution. Chapter 5 concludes with the robustly interrogative intelligence of the founder of Western ethical philosophy, and misses it.

While discussing the vanishing of histories in systems of Western education, Chapter 5 does not enumerate the exact problems that this causes. My final chapter, however, takes a subset of history in general and asks some questions about a topic fraught with peril that is not only hard to discuss but almost impossible to formulate. The subject is what the loss of histories might mean for a contemporary understanding of cultural identity and its relation to migration and the challenge of fundamentalism and nationalism. Or, at least, my chapter ruminates on how difficult it is, for a number of reasons, to ask Socratic questions about this topic and how tough, amid the compound discrediting of almost all pasts, it is to assemble the beginnings of answers.

Throughout *Forgetfulness*, I don't disguise the difficulty—often the impossibility—of evading modernity's chosen habits of forgetfulness. Modernity has had enormous success in categorizing objections to its principles in negative terms and in persuading us not to question them. It is also true that potentially rebellious opportunities and practices are often bought up by modernity itself—*pour encourager les autres*—and reshaped into modernity's own ways and subsumed into its values. The rebels I find in this book, insofar as I do find them, are, nevertheless, intellectually consequential even if they are also, inevitably, gestural and often open to objection.

Chapter 6 begins with some reflections on contemporary ways in which a response to, or frail rebellion against, modernity's ways of forgetfulness has been achieved in words. These acts of resistance are, generally, imaginative and sometimes sentimental. They are periodically lacking in intellectual rigor. But what matters first of all in my chapter is not their credibility but their existence: their indication of further, furtive human aspirations to exist in a different relationship with pasts. My topic is initially modernity in conjunction with rural landscapes, which have provided the scene, so to speak, of felt, if sometimes fabricated, connections to distant pasts. Part of my discussion concerns a cadre of "nature writers" (that is not an adequate term but will have to serve for the moment) who read the landscape as if it were a page from an ancient epic. We are back, in the faintest of terms, to Mycenae. The landscapes in question, in my discussion, are mostly English and occasionally Scottish. But this is not a chapter meant to be exclusive to the countries of the British Union. Surveying some modern writing about the natural world and the scoring of topography by history, I appraise contemporary writers of the countryside—mostly walkers through rural scenes—who have mused on identities through narratives of wild space. I think about how these writers are the faintest, most far-off, inheritors of the old memory cultures of the ancient world.

This topic then prompts me to ask where ideas of the interrelationship between time and place belong amid the modern problem of migration—walking through landscapes of a different kind. The liberal West is bothered about the political implications of its own recent national histories—understandably fearful, in the wake of the Second World War (1939–45)—that national or even local histories are always potentially or actually national*ist*. But, at the same time, modernity has ensured we can barely recall most histories anyway. Our tools, I suggest, for thinking harder about the relationship between places, peoples, and histories in the present troubles generated by fundamentalism and antiliberal nationalism—Europe, not least after "Brexit," is at its most unstable since the 1930s—and the problems of migration could hardly be less adequate. To this chapter I add some brief reflections on another challenge to the idea of history and home in relation to specific *places*, which is the globalization of business and the power of brands to transform cities and towns into more or less exact replicas of each other by ensuring that the same commercial outlets are present across the world. If at one level this multiplication allows us to feel at ease in a plurality of cultures because their high streets look reassuringly the same, it also erodes our sense of urban places as having specific identities, built on and with particular visualities, customs, and pasts.

Forgetfulness is not a formal academic history of the loss of history, or of the history of loss. The book is a composite of historical narration, cultural and literary criticism, opinion, and autobiography. It's also in part about what I remember—or think I do—because that is my local, private, and *inutile* form of resistance to a greater expectation that I should really be thinking about tomorrow. My attempt is to catch in words something of the felt experience of a deracinated modernity and to notice the hidden and not-so-hidden recognition of alternatives or, at least, the resistances and regrets. My book is not disposed to be very optimistic. But I don't think *Forgetfulness* is ever without a pale Fenland hope that looking backward might give us a way of looking ahead more confidently and with more rootedness, not merely to single places or cultures but to life and history themselves. *Forgetfulness* is in praise of valuing, or minimally in simply remembering better, what consequence history has bequeathed to us, of deeds and things. This book's aspiration is Homeric. It is in tribute to keeping in mind the best of pasts—and not getting rid of them.

1

Cultures of memory

"You do stir up in me a longing for my brave comrades,
speaking of unforgettable, unforgettable things [...]"

Xerxes Emperor of the Persians, in AESCHYLUS,
Πέρσαι, *Persae* (472 BC)

Guidebooks stand in for an education some of us did not have. They fill gaps with chatty informality, lending us temporary knowledge we have not forgotten but never acquired. As my girlfriend and I opened the hired Citroën's doors in the dusty car park at Mycenae in the summer of 1994, we were there because our *Rough Guide to Greece* had told us to go. No one had taught me classical Greek, let alone the terms of Mycenaean culture, at my West Midlands comprehensive school. What I knew of the Olympian myths was from children's introductions. I knew how the skyline of Periclean Athens looked from advertisements. Indirectly through English literature I had grasped something of the basics of Greece's most important surviving narratives. The *Rough Guide* had a useful description of the family tree of the House of Atreus. I ought to know about this, I felt, guiltily. The cicadas in the gnarled trees were loud. The heat was almost suffocating.

Fire, recently, had swept across the undergrowth near the ancient palace, a military fortification that 1,500 years before the birth of

Jesus had dominated the southern Greek world: ancient Mycenaean culture. Scorched yellow by the sun, the ground was charred. We walked over the inhospitable soil. A snake, nearly a meter long, broke cover—from whatever half-cremated stalks, holes, and pebbles constituted "cover." The snake, in angry S-like waves, powered ahead. Brown, primitive, fast, it was *Vipera ammodytes*, the most toxic of the European vipers, and one of the European continent's most ancient living species.

Insight has long been associated with such creatures. Here was a carrier of secret knowledge, occult understanding. It possessed, supposedly, the wisdom of the serpent. Judeo-Christian history began with both respect and fear of such beings. The burst of panic we briefly witnessed, nevertheless, had no wisdom. Indeed, it had no clue where it was. The snake did not understand that it was almost on top of the scene—so it has been asserted—of one of ancient Greece's most famous murders. But then, except for the *Rough Guide*'s family tree, neither did I.

Clytemnestra, urged by her lover Aegisthus, slew her husband, Agamemnon, here. (I'm suspending discussions of the relationship between plain and figurative sense, between what the Jewish tradition would call *peshat* and *derash*, in the Greek histories for a moment.) Agamemnon's name, perhaps, means "think about things a lot" and he commanded the eventually victorious Achaean (the old term for the ancient Greeks) armies during the long siege of Troy. That siege was perhaps the single most significant ancient event in the surviving records of the Turkish-Greek-Mycenaean-Mediterranean world. Either Clytemnestra killed Agamemnon with a mesh (perhaps a blanket) and a knife, or Aegisthus did it himself, or they both committed the crime together: sources differ. Entangled like a dolphin in a trawler's net, Agamemnon, in most versions, could neither free nor defend himself. He died.

It has long been forgotten whether this treacherous event, the butchering of a husband by a wife, is historical or imaginary (it ought to be added that Agamemnon had been disloyal to Clytemnestra too: this was not a one-sided moral problem). The founding stories of classical Greece may or may not be true—but then that necessitates a difficult question about what might be meant by true: *peshat* or *derash*. The Greeks, certainly, had a complex and advanced sense of what constituted veracity. It did not merely reside in what was factually certain or empirically demonstrable. If one were to judge Homer or Aeschylus, for instance, simply by the standards of historical accuracy, one would be faced with a reassessment of what constitutes accuracy itself.

In Mycenae in 1994, as my girlfriend and I walked to the small outcrop of scorchingly hot stones, I recognized the ground plan of a palace, the pockmarks on an arid landscape of an ancient habitation. And, closer to the palace walls, I saw deep pits. What were they, I asked? It was as if some embittered archaeologist had left behind crude symbolic representations of what had mostly been done with the past. Thrown into a hole, left in a dark place without a sign to say what it was or a memory to recall it.

I looked at the *Rough Guide*. The sun made the pages painfully white. The grave of Agamemnon, I read. Or, at least, this is what the nineteenth-century German archaeologist Heinrich Schliemann (1822–90) thought.

No one remembers whether the House of Atreus is real or otherwise. But Schliemann—a businessman as well as a despoiler of ancient tombs, who made a fortune out of military contracts from the Crimean War (1853–6)—either believed he had found Clytemnestra's victim or thought that fame would come from asserting that he had. The archaeologist had either obtained evidence that Agamemnon was real or he was roguishly endeavoring to lend him a corporeality he never possessed. I could not judge. Schliemann's team dug into the burial site in the rain in November 1876. And at the bottom, after a weekend off, they encountered a royal sepulcher. The body had long gone. But the mask protecting the head had not. "I have today," Schliemann is alleged to have declared, "gazed on the face of Agamemnon."

Had he?

Here, Schliemann claimed, was a momentous survival from what other people thought a legend. Schliemann had named his son Agamemnon and his daughter Andromache. Yet he had also fathered a dispute, a contention about the historical authenticity of what he had exhumed in the rain of the Peloponnese a year before Queen Victoria's Ruby Jubilee. In the absence of memory, queries and uncertainties creep up even as, sometimes, hard facts return.

Studying Schliemann's mask on display in the National Archaeological Museum in Athens, I wondered if anyone would ever know what it was. Would there be a future point when it was established for sure whether this treasure, made from solid gold, belonged to one of the most significant narratives in the surviving antique histories of Western humanity? There is some evidence to imply that the mask long predates the period traditionally associated with the Trojan War. But there is also an argument which says that those traditional dates are wrong and that the events described in the *Odyssey* and *Iliad* relate to a period far more remote than the age in which Homer's narratives were written down. And Homer himself, as Adam Nicolson reminds us, is a figure of speech, not a human being. Homer's true starting point may be much more ancient than we understand. "No man called Homer was ever known," Nicolson says, "and it doesn't help to think of Homer as a man. Easier and better is to see him abstractly, as the collective and inherited vision of great acts done long ago." My book might be thought as a brief exploration of the implications, in general terms, of that adroit observation. There are other, more mundane, claims that Schliemann slipped an artifact into the tomb from another dig, as the fraudulent ghost-buster Harry Price (1881–1948) made up evidence that Borley Rectory was England's most haunted house in the middle of the 1930s. History is not without its pretenders.

There is no agreement about the mask. A flat, lifeless face cut in gold in a museum case. It struck me, as I looked, that it was not unlike a German patrician from the 1870s. There was a hint of an Otto von Bismarck moustache. Could Schliemann have simply *forged it*?

If I remembered the grave of Agamemnon at Mycenae later, was I recollecting a hard historical fact from the dawn of modern Europe? Or was I recalling the product of a nineteenth-century businessman's delusion? I did not know. Schliemann had been obsessed enough to baptize his children with chanted words from the *Iliad*. I gazed into the hole, wondering what I was seeing. Then I looked over the charred Attic ground where the snake had traveled. Above me was the luminous sky. It was like a holiday advert for a week in Greece. This book about forgetfulness, with its exploration of what we cannot recall, started in that blazing sun of the northeastern Peloponnese. It commenced its life—at least I think I am right in remembering this—among ancient graves of almost-forgotten origin, and with stories that no one can recollect any longer whether they are true.

It was a peculiarly appropriate place, now I see, in which to begin. That is because the ancient Mediterranean deplored what slipped from the mind. And the meanings of modern forgetfulness can be grasped with clarity, I think, by comparing them to the work of memory in ancient Europe, of which I briefly take Mycenae as representative. The "back story" of modern forgetfulness has two principal parts, which I explore here. One is the memory culture of the ancient

West. The other is the transformation of that culture's understanding of time by Christianity.

*   *   *

European antiquity conceptualized forgetfulness in terms our world, the ideas that constitute our Western present, can barely comprehend. In Mycenae today, the visitor stands at a historical site that (perhaps) provided a core narrative that all educated Athenians, all educated Greeks in general, would have known. Whether these narratives are literally true or otherwise is not, here, the point. Invented or empirical, they were always—so far as we understand—to be remembered. These were family sagas that not only bore retelling but also required it.

The history of the House of Atreus, to take one saga, is first glimpsed in Homeric texts that were possibly first written down—language analysts suggest—at the beginning of the eighth century before the birth of Jesus. We do not know how many centuries previously the oral tradition had begun. The same narratives were performed on the Athenian stage four centuries later. They were echoed in Rome by Vergil (70–19 BC) in the *Aeneid* just a few decades before Jesus's birth. These were plots that survived across centuries, most likely through more than a millennium.

Why were these stories remembered? It was because the culture, as well as the political, theological, and ethical life, of Greece was peculiarly averse to forgetfulness. Ancient Greece distinguished between two different forms of time: *chronos* (the simple succession of events) and *kairos* (the moment of consequence, the point at which something of significance occurs). If *chronos* was easily to be forgotten (when exactly *did* the Fall of Troy occur? Homer, for one, is bad on dates), *kairos* was certainly not. In the memory of great deeds, the recognition of past events of consequence—given permanent literary form in, for instance, Homer's epics—human beings discerned their principal source of meaning and stability.

Committed, in due course, to the honor of ancestors and in perpetual hope of their assistance, the remotest human communities, long prior to the mature civilizations of Greece and Rome, preserved, it is hypothesized, a living sense of the presence of history. History's reality was here and now. It's inferred, as Larry Siedentop points out in *Inventing the Individual: The Origins of Western Liberalism* (2014), that the first human social units were built around the family. These units have left no written trace. But, like the hypothesized language of Indo-European, something can be gleaned, something tentatively reconstructed, from descendants.

Within that family cell it is likely that there were rigidly fixed gender expectations. There were, most probably, predetermined hierarchies of power in general. The purpose of this book is not directly to defend these. The purpose in adducing the structures of the ancient world is, rather, to point up, via a contrast, the distinctiveness of our own assumptions about time and history. What is of interest among the values of the remotest European cultures are the suggestive implications of a continual and continued devotion to vital histories, to ancestors whose protection and displeasure were, respectively, craved and feared. These values set the terms, established the foundations of rules and regulations, of the earliest human groups to which we can have (some) access, and their relation to time. What gradually occurred in the history of societal development, as much as it is now comprehended, was the slow expansion of these small family units into larger ones: into extended families, then into hamlets, villages, towns, and finally into cities. But the governing principles did not essentially alter. The family rules developed into the guiding conditions of what we can now call, in shorthand, the πόλις (*polis*)—the city as the source of citizenship.

Within the elongated but specific structures of the ancient *polis*, with its own gods, traditions, and rites, a citizen's place and responsibilities were clear. This was in essence the same as, long before, all family members' had been. Clear and unchallengeable, too, were the social locations, duties, responsibilities, and dangers of those who were not citizens: women, minors, slaves. Only in the *polis*, the home city, could a citizen—by definition a male—properly worship. In turn, only in his home place could the citizen avoid dishonoring, and therefore being punished by, his household gods. With the *polis* as the conceptual basis for order and meaning, the ancient Mediterranean invented the idea of the country: it was that which was *contra* the *polis* (to mix languages): the wilderness, the opposite of arrangement, sense, and plan.

Solely in his own city could the citizen retain harmony with his ancestors whose goodwill he cultivated. The past could not be forgotten. It was barely recognized as past. Only in the *polis* was such a man, paying what was due to his local ancestral divinities, able to live out the existence intended for him in, as he believed, an ordered universe. The *polis* gave the citizen a role and an identity. It was a microcosm of the structured *cosmos* in which he understood he lived, and which the *polis*—as he thought—replicated at a sublunary level. Obeying the rules of his own city, the citizen was able to be the person he was meant to be.

Such principles, for the purposes of this book, defined a memory culture, a way of existing in a community where shared assumptions about history and the vigor of continuations were necessary. To forget here was to destroy. It is worth, certainly, remembering Freud's alternative perspective on such early communities in *Civilization and Its Discontents* (1930), his assessment of the fact that the great enemy of civilization is humanity's natural tendency to violence. Here, Freud dwelt on the obvious fact that the citizen's right to express himself came at a cost. "[Let] us not forget," Freud said of primitive man, "that in the primeval family only its head could give full rein to his drives; its members lived in slavish suppression." But in terms of the mental furniture of such early life, we can see, however much Freud is right, securities. To attend to the past faithfully was to ensure safety; to fulfill one's obligations to history was to cement one's relationship with the present as something grounded in and by the past. And, conversely, it was clear when an attitude to time was dangerous. To overlook one's ancestors, for example, was to incur peril from their hypervigilant wrath. To omit to honor one's gods was to invite vengeance. And revenge is the dark side of a culture that cannot forget.

Failure to recall the *polis* and its traditions was, in addition, to declare oneself not only a traitor but also a nonperson. Rebels were the antagonists of memory. And in turn they were enemies of the society's best values. Such unconscionable, mutinous forgetfulness was a form of suicide. In fact, it was something more terrible than that. For the ancient world, with its faith in the living continuations of the remembered, there was a fate worse than death.

The loss of the *polis* was annihilation. And so exile was more dreadful than execution. The banished citizen became a no-man, a creature without an identity because he was outwith a structuring, defining society. The exile was the etiolated wanderer of a foreign landscape, multiply displaced from, and *contra*, who he was and ought to be. Back within the *polis* that had cast him out, the exile was only to be remembered because he might try to return. Someone had to recollect his face because if he did come back, it was necessary to know whom to kill. And such extermination was, within these terms, a relief.

The founding myth of Rome, the narrative of the establishment of the imperial capital as Greece's inheritor and summation (as the Romans desired to think), is given shape in Vergil's *Aeneid*. That is the Latin answer to the epics of Homer. And Vergil's epic amply reveals, a few years before the beginning of the Christian era, the continuation of ancient faiths in continuations. Rome inherits Greece (or at least asserts that she does). And that inheritance, along with the statues, politics, gods, and wine, includes fundamental intuitions. The *Aeneid* is, in turn, as committed to the work of memory against the curse of forgetting as any surviving text from the peoples of the ancient Mediterranean.

Vergil's unfinished epic restates the grounding assumptions of a remembrance culture. And it makes clear what such a culture's consolations, duties, and fears are. The *Aeneid* narrates the wandering of the Trojan Aeneas—son of the Dardanian Prince Anchises and the goddess Venus (Aphrodite in Greece), a mix of the empirical and the spiritual—and his companions after their city has been destroyed by the Achaean armies. The great catastrophe of the ancient classical West governed by the concept of the *polis*—the loss of home—is squarely confronted. Revealingly, Vergil requested that this epic be destroyed, some reports say, after his death. He asked, allegedly, that the *Aeneid* be obliterated because the poet had not finished it. Vergil seemingly could not contemplate an incomplete epic about completion, a text that described a continuation that was not itself continued. The poet's orders, assuming the story is true, were fortunately disregarded.

A salute to traditions and that which must never be lost, Vergil's hexameters are fraught with the anguish of nearly vanishing. Exiled from the *polis*, Aeneas and his men travel slowly from the destroyed Troy, experiencing a number of disappointments, temptations, and mistakes, to the site of what will eventually become the Eternal City of Rome. There, guided by the gods, they build the new Troy. It is, Vergil says, the old reborn. Aeneas and his followers achieve this restoration—or rather continuation—because of what they have, materially, retrieved from the burning walls of their original home. They have their memories of Troy that periodically make Aeneas

weep in near-despair at his bereavement. But his combat with the terror of the forgotten, the awfulness of exile, involves hard objects too.

Aeneas and his companions transport their household gods, the
votive statues of the principal guardians of their Trojan hearths. They
carry, in addition, the immortal fire that preserves symbolically the
essence of Troy—a fiery Ark of the Covenant, the figurative rainbow
that does not promise renewal but is renewal's living substance. "Troy
entrusts to you her holy things and household gods," Aeneas is told by
Hector's phantom as he, Aeneas, prepares to abandon the fallen city.
Hector's comforting speech—the great warrior Hector, if anyone, can
speak for Troy—continues:

> ["]hos cape fatorum comites, his moenia quaere
> magna pererrato statues quae denique ponto."
> sic ait et manibus uittas Vestamque potentem
> aeternumque adytis effert penetralibus ignem.

In H. Rushton Fairclough's elegant translation, this reads: " 'Take them
[your companions] to share your fortunes: seek for them the mighty
city, which, when you have wandered over the deep, you shall at last
establish.' So [Hector] speaks and in his hands brings forth from the
inner shrine the [crowns], great Vesta, and the undying fire." The
empirical embodiment of an unbroken tradition, here is the element
(literally) that secures Troy's survival as something more than an idea
or a memory despite her devastation.

The *Aeneid* is restorative. It is an *Ur*-text of recuperation, of the
rejection or bypassing of forgetfulness. The epic tells us that forced
exile need not be exile forever, even if the sorrows of waiting for a new
home are nearly overwhelming. The poem is a legitimation myth, too,
which seeks to graft the new city of Rome onto the ancient lineage of
an earlier noble *polis* (Geoffrey of Monmouth would endeavor to do
exactly the same for London, "Troia Nova," in his fanciful chronicle

Historia Regum Britanniae (c.1136)). Rome is not only a place but also a concept; not only new but also a living recollection, a vitalized reconstitution, of a past. Vergil's epic is an exemplary narrative of a memory culture that can only move forward when it builds on its history.

Christianity came to the ancient world shortly after Vergil died. And here is the second key element in the broadest context of remembering and forgetting in the contemporary West. Early Christianity, not least in its Latin and Anglo-Saxon forms, transformed the idea of the *polis* as continuation into a faith in a hoped-for union with a God who was always everywhere: who did not, by definition, reside in a single location. Proposing a ubiquitous single (though also Trinitarian) divinity, the new faith rendered obsolete an imperative term of the ancient memory culture. The principal fault line in the West's movement from remembering to looking ahead begins in earnest in Bethlehem.

Being an exile from the remembered, from the *polis* and all its traditions and continuations, makes no sense in Christianity. The disciples of Jesus, who told His followers in John 18:36 that "my kingdom is not of this world," encouraged believers to consider not the unbroken continuations of an ancestral past but to concentrate on the living presence of an undestroyable and ever-present God. The Father was not of this world, though He intervened in it, and certainly not of a single city or people. Splintering the conception of human life based on sustaining the ways of a localizable past, Trinitarian Christianity, particularly in its eschatology, altered human beings' relationship with time (and, in turn, with place).

The new faith, what must have seemed first of all a new Middle Eastern cult of the son of Joseph the Carpenter, not only discouraged acts of devotion to what had happened long ago in the manner of the *polis* but also explicitly reorientated its followers' minds to the future. Eternal life and the union of the soul with the divine at

death—although hardly discussed in the collection of sacred scriptures agreed as canonical by the beginning of the fifth century—
became a new aspiration. Christianity was not unique in proposing
the possibility of eternal life. The Greeks had a concept of it (see, for
instance, Euripides's *Alcestis* or Book XI of the *Odyssey*) and so did
the Romans—not least as we learn from Book VI of the *Aeneid* when
Aeneas visits the underworld and meets the shade both of his lover
Dido and his unembraceable father. In the northern lands, the Norse
religions had a conception of an enduring reward for the brave after
death, too. But Christianity, offering the notion of a blissful eternity
for all faithful men and women, was distinctive not least in its intense
concentration on hope's possibility, on the chance of conquering the
tomb for all those steadfast in their belief. Expectation and anticipation assumed the mental space previously occupied by the duties of
remembering.

Christianity has its own respect for the past. It has, for a start,
those canonical sacred narratives that must not be forgotten even
if, in terms of the Old and New Testaments, it has found multiple
ways of altering the meaning of the former (itself not agreed) to
cohere with the meaning (itself not agreed) of the latter. Yet the
focus on what was to come was different from the thought systems
from which the Christian faith emerged. And alongside that concentration of the future was also, in the practices of Christianity,
instructive rites for rejecting history. In its formal acts of penitence,
for example, Christianity proposed a way of blotting out the past,
understood as the scene of sin. Forgiveness erased the unwanted
events of yesterday. Absolved, the Christian could aspire to a future
where he or she would, it was to be hoped, live better. This is strik-
ingly in conflict with the ancient concept of revenge, the legitimacy
of which is debated, for instance, in Aeschylus's *Oresteia*: a form of
justice predicated on the impossibility of overlooking what had once

been done. What ousted revenge in Christian ethics (cf. Romans 12:19) was broadly the chance to move on through absolution, a practice of forgetting and forgiving the past, or at least of leaving justice to the Father.

St Augustine's *The City of God* (426) is among the important early texts about the Christian erasure of history in preference for that which is to come. It is an extended study, moving Pauline Christianity from the ancient thought-world by reorienting human beings from history to futurity, from remembering to hoping. Augustine's life as a convert, as a believer who rejected, like St Paul, his own past, helped assure him that the future was better than history: of his own, Augustine was publicly ashamed (though also complicatedly absorbed). In place of that old Mediterranean idea of where the citizen's identity came from, Augustine declared, is a new eternal city that is home to a Christian wherever he or she is. His title, *De ciuitate Dei contra paganos* (*The City of God against the Pagans*), is really "the Christian city against the ancient *polis.*" The assumptions of ancient Greece and Rome and the lost cultures from which they inherited were upturned. "The glorious city of God is my theme in this work," Augustine said in Marcus Dods's translation:

> I have undertaken its defense against those who prefer their own gods to the Founder of this city,—a city surpassingly glorious, whether we view it as it still lives by faith in this fleeting course of time, and sojourns as a stranger in the midst of the ungodly, or as it shall dwell in the fixed stability of its eternal seat, which it now with patience waits for, expecting until "righteousness shall return unto judgment," and it obtain, by virtue of its excellence, final victory and perfect peace.

There is neither isolation nor exile from traditions and unbroken continuities conceivable here. And such continuities are no longer what matters. Wherever he or she stands, the Christian is in the presence of God. He or she neither honors a local divinity nor looks to private or limited traditions, grounded in a particular location. And, with the ubiquity of the Father's existence, the Christian is discouraged from prioritizing devotions to the past because he or she regards primarily the future. There will be, for the righteous, what Augustine calls "final victory and perfect peace." Security and value are not to be discovered in a prolongation of history. They are, rather, to be desired from its ending.

Augustine advised his readers to break from the past and look both to the skies and the future. It was a critical moment in the establishment of the intellectual conditions of the modern world.

"If Homer had remained our Bible," said Johann Wolfgang von Goethe (1749–1832), "what a different aspect humanity would have had!" In the story of the making of modern forgetfulness, Goethe could not have been more correct.

2

The making of modern forgetting

"Everybody in the crowded street, it seemed, had some end in view. Everybody was hurrying along to keep some appointment."
VIRGINIA WOOLF, "1880," *The Years* (1937)

It is apt that one of the places of European modernity—a location that played a pivotal role in shifting the contemporary West's relationship with time—is a city. It is neither a theoretical *polis* nor the conceptual City of God but a real and earthly place: Paris. Within the capital of France, there is one public square that peculiarly embodies the intensity of modern Europe's relationship with history and dominant modern conceptions of chronological direction. Here indeed is a site of *kairos* rather than *chronos*, though *chronos*—the matter of what literally happened—is important too. Christianity began the process of moving us toward the future. The French Revolution from 1789 to 1815 (which was, ironically enough, violently antagonistic to Christianity as belonging to the past) clinched, not least in that square, secular expectations about the relative values of tomorrow over yesterday.

Wait at the Place de la Concorde in the eighth *arrondissement*, with the Tour Eiffel in view, beside the grand Hôtel de Crillon. Times coincide in one very obvious way here. In the same direction that the nineteenth-century marvel of the Eiffel Tower (which opened in March 1889) is visible, so is the ancient obelisk of the Egyptian pharaoh Ramesses II. This is a huge ornamental artifact from the ancient world in the center of a modern European roundabout. Ramesses, sometimes known as Ozymandias (of whom Shelley wrote) died in 1213 BC. Time is synchronized or at least collapsed, as if it has hastened by at an eye-watering pace. And, appropriately, the unavoidable impression around the pharaoh's monument, with its intricate hieroglyphs few now can read, is usually of speed: of competing vehicles—cars, vans, motorcycles, even the occasional crazy cyclist—circumnavigating the multilane island. The traffic passes in haste up toward or down from the Champs-Élysées, one of the most headlong of the central Parisian routes. Named after the Hellenic Elysian fields, the pastures of Paradise, it is a long time since asphodel grew here.

Speed, as well as a more fundamental change in the comprehension of time, became visible in this square in 1789. The violent revelation in Paris that year was that social and political structures could be overthrown; that revolution could, at least theoretically, not merely revise but transform the established order. The French Revolution, with its complex intellectual, social, economic, and political causes, is the emblematic occurrence in the modern shaping of European ideas of time. The Revolution required the substantial rethinking of ideas about the security of the present and the possibilities of alteration to come. It obliged a new mental understanding of a human being's relationship with the clock and the calendar (which, as it happens, Napoleon Bonaparte (1769–1821) rewrote).

Revolutions had occurred in Europe and beyond before and so had Civil War. Great Britain had executed her own monarch (Charles I) in January 1649 as France would execute Louis XVI, in this square, in January 1793. Great Britain had too, in something like a fit of absence of mind, lost the colonies of North America (and not thought that was too important) in what was understood in America, then eventually in Great Britain, as a revolution. But the pace of change in the years 1789–1815 in France altered more thoroughly European understanding of how an individual might relate to the past, to what could now be comprehended as old orders that were not, it turned out, permanent. "It is difficult," says the late cultural theorist Benedict Anderson with a sensible observation in *Imagined Communities: Reflections on the Origin and Spread of Nationalism* (1983, revised 1991), "to recreate in the imagination a condition of life in which [a] nation was felt to be something utterly new." That was true of the United States after the Declaration of Independence in 1776. And it was also almost true of revolutionary France after 1789. That upheaval, far from the assumptions of the ancient *polis*, made every adult a *citoyen(ne)* who could, in principle, assist in determining the new direction of a nation state. What was "France" had, at the level of an idea, changed.

The tumultuous period rendered clear the conceptualization of "the past" as that which was different from the present and, potentially, the future. *L'ancien régime*, the old order, apparently crumbed away, even though it shortly came back in a different guise. The French Revolution was a conflict that, it turned out, ended up confirming something like the previous *status quo*. Despite the turmoil, France moved from an absolute monarchy to an empire to a restored monarchy via an only briefly experienced republic. France, then as now, could not decide whether radicalism should lead to fundamental change or not. Yet the violent convulsions of political transformation centered on Paris from 1789 till the Battle of Waterloo just outside Brussels on June 18, 1815, disclosed to nineteenth-century Europe that, in principle at least, men and women could adjust their relationship to history by their own determined, and, if necessary, bloody, intervention. Time, it was confirmed, was not static but dynamic.

Standing by the Place de la Concorde, the "place of harmony," is to feel something of the way in which an idea of harmony can be imposed by changing words. This is a forum, now often a traffic jam, that has variously been shaped and variously been named to represent the people of France, the nation state, and her future. The square's history captures France's brutal story, and her attempts to forget it, through the spectacles that occurred within this space just as the alterations of its name record the principal events of relatively recent Parisian history. This public square, originally created in 1755 in the last decades of the Old Order, was first known, with honorable respect to the reigning monarch, as *Place Louis XV*. In the turmoil 40 or so years later, its new name signified, as the *Place de la Révolution*, that *l'ancien régime* was over and its traces were being erased. Freedom fighters now occupied the heart of Paris not least because they occupied, and renamed, this square. In the episodes that occurred here, the *Place* indicated how the revolutionaries dealt with the literal representatives of former things and, then, with each other, in a kind of bloodbath of excision, a compulsory obliteration of previous ways of being. The *Place de la Révolution* was the cradle of national carnage, the site of the guillotine that was used to execute Louis XVI, Louis XV's grandson. Here, too, Marie Antoinette, Louis XVI's queen, perished. The *Place* became the symbolic location that figured the capacity of the French people to rebel against the seemingly natural, God-given structures of history and established power.

The *polis* was now the political; the scene not of continuation but overthrow. And the material, technological history of the first half of the nineteenth century did nothing but accelerate the comprehension of time as mobile, of the future as something that could be expected to involve (advantageous) change. Transformation seeped into modern consciousness as part of what it meant to be alive. The alteration in Europe's understanding of its relationship with history suggested by the Revolution was extended, and complicated, by machines and inventions, technology and technology's influence on human expectations. The material history of modernity, in short, concerns the increasing centrality of futures—different kinds of revolution, but ones that similarly insisted on the value of moving away from older things and which helped identify progress, in the sense of the rejection of the past and the privileging of the unhappened, as needful.

It is easy to overlook the significance and complexity of European roads prior to the Industrial Revolution. They had their own tightly scheduled transport systems and the network of communications they made possible. Yet it was the glamour, and energy, of steam power that transformed not only transport but also a general sense of what could be achieved within a given space of time. Roads mattered. Yet the railways changed them. Steam made traveling but also harvesting, spinning, weaving, plowing, and manufacturing in general quicker and more uniform. It made printing on paper faster and the distribution of views more rapid (a relevant issue for political revolutionaries, apart from anyone else, as, for instance, the role of journalists and the printing press in the Hungarian revolution of 1848-9 rendered clear). And as steam power revolutionized urban and rural labor in general, it created industrial manufacturing that slowly—though not *that* slowly—began to categorize "manual work" as low grade. The new technology shifted the class status of effort. With developments in automated machinery, in turn, the desire to compete—that peculiarly monetized way of regarding the future—intensified. Robert Moore, Charlotte Brontë's manufacturer in her political novel *Shirley* (1849), waits for new machines for his cotton mill, which require far fewer hands to work them. "Mr. Moore loved his machinery," Brontë's narrator reflects: "He had risked the last of his capital on the purchase of these frames and shears which to-night had been expected. Speculations most important to his interests depended on the results to be wrought by them." Charlotte Brontë was not wrong to imagine that this was the speculating voice of the future, about the future.

Steam also made the movement of men and women, as well as of commodities, soldiers, and weapons, swifter. During the 1840s, boiling water accelerated the systems by which men and women traveled around on land as well as at sea. The SS *Savannah*, the first ocean-going trans-Atlantic steamship, undertook the first crossing from one shore to the other in the early summer of 1819, only 4 years after the French Revolutionary Wars had concluded. The steam train derived from technology developed in the years before the Revolution but, in the United Kingdom, became viable as a mode of transportation with the success of the English engineer George Stephenson's *Rocket* in 1829. A year later, the Liverpool and Manchester Railway opened for business to both passengers and freight. The railway, symbolically as well as in practical life, became a signifier of modernity. By the mid-century, it was a necessity.

Transport accelerated the orientation of minds toward futurity. As the lines connected parts of the United Kingdom to each other as never before (the same was happening in portions of continental Europe and North America), the railways obliged the standardization of time. And they created a new attentiveness to it, a new way of understanding what a minute and its passing meant. Railway schedules could not operate with local times as they existed across the United Kingdom at the commencement of the nineteenth century (only Christ Church, Oxford, retains a local time in the United Kingdom today, being 5 minutes behind standard time). Those schedules required precision and consistency. No one who journeyed on the trains could be unaware of the significance of a few (standardized) minutes. A traveler became acquainted with the now familiar business of keeping an eye on the clock. A train, then as now, could be caught or missed on the basis of seconds. Planning ahead to the minute was part of the newly exciting but also fretful experience of locomotion.

The railways imparted vitality to ways of collapsing or "speeding up" time. And they also helped in the privileging of what is new or next above what had already happened. Marcel Proust understood the excitement of this. But there was, more obviously, that which was troublesome. A train that has departed is of no interest. No one, then as now, looks down the track to see the trains they have failed to catch—except, perhaps, to berate themselves for being late. They look more urgently up the track to see whether the next one is visible. The train timetable, the use of schedules to manage traveling life to the second, emerged here as what we can now retrospectively perceive as the new commercial document of futurity, encouraging passengers to assess the shortest wait for what was still to come. The railway station in turn established itself as quintessentially the modern place of passage, the space defined by what was to happen next, a prime feature of the *Einstellung*—the mechanized, rigid forms of thinking—of the new world. Not a destination in itself but a location to leave, either in or out, the railway station clinched the transitionary, the migratory, the peripatetic nature of the citizenry of modernity, saluting the promise of what was going presently to occur, or where we were going next.

The trains of the early and mid-nineteenth century accelerated the development of the telegraph even as they also speeded up its competitor: the postal service. Here was the first major development of high-speed communication that would, over the space of a few decades, shift what men and women could say to each other and how. The telegraph was the starting point of what has become, more than a century and a half later, the instantaneous world of "real-time" transmissions that focus our attention on what the short-term future will bring. Telegraphy gradually acclimatized the mind to a technology that rendered its user impatient: it nourished anticipation. As a man or woman waited for a promptly transmitted message to be answered, he or she learned what we now expect from multiple systems of electronic communication: an answer soon. A few hours, in the world of telegraphy, became a weight of slowed-down time.

Sending concise messages along the train line to import or accept instructions commenced in London in the 1830s. News of delays, after some refinement in the technology and the codes telegraphy employed, could soon be passed along the trackside wires rapidly. Telegraphy, in this environment, supported better regulated assistance in times of need and allowed for accidents and timetable changes to be reported quickly. But this was only a local application of a new technology for modern transport that sent words humming through cables faster than the trains themselves traveled. The cables really did hum, by the way, so that it became possible for poets to describe, to *hear*, how modernity sounded; what noise newness made.

In the United States, Samuel Morse (1791–1872) patented his electrical telegraph in 1837. He transmitted a celebrated message using his shortly-to-be-patented system of dots and dashes, "What hath God wrought," from the Capitol to Baltimore in 1841. Shortly afterward, Morse Code became the largely undisputed language of telegraphy, which would presently connect New York to London by submarine cable. Morse Code is still in use, of course, and was updated most recently in 2004 with the addition of a code for "@," a neat overlapping of the old communication system with the new. (The code needed for the transmission of anyone's email address or Twitter handle is · – – · – ·.) By the 1870s, London could communicate with New Zealand and the huge landmass of the Indian subcontinent through overland and undersea wires. The management of empire depended on these telegraphic cables and so did rebellion against the empire. Indeed, the telegraph made it possible to speak of remotely "managing" at all. Telegraphy altered the world, confirming how quickly change could occur, how rapidly news could be communicated as well as instruction. It more generally groomed men and women to attend primarily on what was to come, to relabel the "recent" as the "out-of-date," to frame the next communication as the more important and the last one in need of updating.

The stock markets, with their eye on the future, depended on telegraphy. And by the end of the nineteenth century, the brokers spoke to each other by the near-instantaneous transmission of the telephone— the first commercial telephone business began in 1877 in the United States. Technology enabled the internationalization of business and the emergence of what could be properly called a global market. Waking each morning, brokers were able to determine what had been happening while they slept. A network of speculators assembled, each endeavoring to comprehend the next direction of this market or that in almost real time. We can obtain this knowledge now from the "stocks app" on smart phones. But that app is not *so* much more rapid than the systems available at the close of the nineteenth century for monitoring and intervening in markets. The speed of communication, and the promise of its developing rapidity, stoked up the understanding, here as elsewhere, that what was around the corner was of peculiar allure. Tomorrow, the next few hours, even the next few minutes, might make or break a sale, improve or damage an income, create or close a job.

By the time of telephony more or less real-time transmission had been achieved. Communication technology, powered by steam, fossil fuels, and electricity, facilitated a previously unheard-of immediacy— though it is true that the actual term, "real time," came into the English language late in the day, as if in ironic tension with the promptness it described. "Real time" is first documented only in the computer age in 1946.

The concept of "next" might seem to imply a sequence. Speaking of "what's next" could appear to indicate a narrative of cause and effect, a teleology, and that what is to come is the natural corollary of what has already happened. But what is next, as the nineteenth century understood it, did not need to belong in a narrative: it did not need to have its roots in history at all. What is next, the Victorian experience revealed, became important in itself, whether that "next" was related to what was already known or otherwise. As the age acclimatized itself to futurity, the excitement as well as the risk of what might happen increased. And this was regardless of the relationship between the new and what had previously occurred. What was fresh or surprising did not have to belong to an ongoing, consecutive pattern; there was no requirement for "the next thing" to fit a sequence of events as a natural corollary. Being new, escaping from any notion of plot or narrative, was enough.

This was most obvious in the transformed sense, in the nineteenth century, of what the "news" looked like. *OED* suggests that the first use of "news" to refer to the reporting of events was in 1417. But this medieval conception—in the year in which the Great Western Schism ended—altered when it became possible to report events more or less as they were happening. How long did it take for knowledge of the death in 1417 of the Antipope Benedict XIII that ended the Great Schism to travel from Avignon to London? How long did clergy in Rome have to wait before finding out that the era of two popes was over? It is hard for the contemporary world to comprehend just how late medieval news could be. The news in the nineteenth century, on the other hand, was the progeny of technologized speed, the offspring of near-simultaneity. *The Times*, for instance, was able from the mid-century onward to include reports from special correspondents

(*OED* dates the term to 1821) sent "by telegram" and often was able to update with new editions during the day with the most recently received wire (though it is worth noting that governments struggled to keep the cost of telegraphy down and it was still, at the end of the century, a relatively expensive way of sending information). This speed allowed for readers of print media to feel part of the ongoing development of the news more or less as it was happening though telegraphy, of course, also meant that mistakes and misunderstandings, to say nothing of deliberate distortions, could circulate before any correcting or interrogating update: rumor and propaganda were propagated by swiftness as much as news.

"Modernity" has been traced in periods of history prior to the nineteenth century. The European Renaissance, the medieval and ancient classical world, the seventeenth and eighteenth centuries: each has been described as involving a distinctive form of modernity. *OED* finds that noun first in print in English in 1635. But its fullest and most exact sense, when "modernity" signifies something more than only the "new," refers to sensations and apprehensions of time pressing forward into the future as a matter of excitement and desire. "Modernity," properly comprehended, is a state of mind that is expectant of, and values, change: here is the recategorization of "alteration" as "fashion." *Kairos* ceases to be a category that refers to what of significance *has* happened and is, instead, a hope for what can be expected from the future. And this modernity-of-mind becomes apparent in Europe and the United States in the nineteenth century. This is modernity as an experience; as a set of pulsations and ways of feeling. It is a category of being, and of being excited (with all its attendant narratives of loss and disappointment) about the new. Modernity is created by the apprehension of time speeding-up and the heightened consciousness of what might happen next. In this modernity, a notion dependent on discontinuities rather than continuations, men and women register the passage of days and hours as the bringer of difference—a kind of revolutionary experience of the dislocation of history apprehended in ordinary urban and suburban life.

The citizens of nineteenth-century modernity comprehend that what is valuable, as well as potentially dangerous, is that which had not yet happened. What is important, to which we should direct our minds, is what that we are on the verge of. Modernity is peculiarly a border state-of-mind; a waiting to go over the edge of the present moment. It cements, as a corollary of this, the conception that there is such a thing called "history" in the simplest sense of a past that is different from the present and the future to come. The experience of modernity exists in an intense expectation of, as well as an (often financialized) desire for, change as well as an anxiety about its failure. It is the conceptual offspring of revolution and a believer in the tiredness of the past.

Modernity privileges what "catches on" (a phrase first recorded in Great Britain and Ireland in 1884 as modernity is in full swing). And, in turn, it tries to guess what will "catch on" next, or at least spends time looking forward to it. Modernity's companions, the modes in which modernity is most visibly articulated, are fashion and the latest style, however this is understood. Modernity is made from the spectacle of the next and the promised—from ideas to shoes.

The nineteenth century, symptomatically, is the period in which the professional advertiser emerges. He (and later she) is an advocate as well as an agent of the "latest thing," a figure peculiarly of industrial modernity. The advertiser provided, then as now, conspicuous encouragement, as well as subliminal and covert encouragement, to consumers to buy. He helped turn people *into* consumers, with their eye on what they could have next. He pressed them to care about what they did not yet possess, encouraging the acquisitive desires on which commodity capitalism depends. Laboring to create new markets, advertisers aspire to generate new "needs," to alter our sense of what we would like into a belief that we are entitled to it or required to have it. Advertisers are figures in the marketplace who advise—sometimes with the illusion of whispering privately to—the citizens of modernity that this product or that is fashionable, and therefore nearly obligatory. They tell us, or seductively permit us to infer, that a commitment to purchasing the new is necessary to be modern. Correspondingly, advertisers intensify the language of the "out-of-date" for what is not "modern," for what has been bought or valued in the past. In the service of consumer culture, advertisers are the imaginative champions of moving on.

The desirable becomes glossier. And the literal experience of shopping (a word that comes into English in 1757) in nineteenth- and early twentieth-century Europe and the United States became *glassier*. Technical developments enhanced the excitement and the simple visibility of searching for the new. The invention of the plate-glass shop window created a kind of theater of consumerism, a way literally of looking that was new—at the new. And it was joined by other developments: the transformation of the single-level market into the department store (department stores began properly in the 1830s); the cognate development of the shopping arcade (the Burlington Arcade opened in London in 1819; the Arcade in Providence, Rhode Island, commenced in 1828): each is a significant moment in the material history of modernity that lies behind the West's complex and extended absorption with looking, and looking ahead. At the close of the nineteenth century, in the material history of shopping, came the escalator and the availability of high-powered electric lighting. These further assisted in the metamorphosis of buying and selling into a scene of social performance. The stalls of the new, the malls of modernity, began literally to glow. Shopping emerged as a fresh form of middle-class self-expression, an assertion of identity and individuality in a context where consumers were encouraged to want what they did not yet have.

Modernity's expectation, even expressed in dress, is that a man or a woman is of the moment. The fashionable is something to live for. Modernity creates a glittering sense of up-to-the-minuteness, of *de nous jours*, even as it encourages a corresponding relabeling of that which is not up-to-the-minute as flabbily "old fashioned." As soon as a culture embraced what was innovative or fresh on this scale, it of necessity recast what was not new, what belonged to last year, or even last week, in uncomplimentary terms. Modernity's lexicon of history's rejection includes, for instance, the idea of being "behind the times" (a term first recorded in 1826). Modernity propelled the language of the "redundant" into a conception of the past, even the history of a shirt or a plate. It invited men and women to believe that things over or old were unimportant, retrogressive, and unsellable.

Tomorrow could make the present better or at least more noticeable. And the nineteenth century understood that securing improvements promised in the days to come was increasingly a matter of individual responsibility—and respectability. Samuel Smiles (1812–1904), the British theorist of middle-class values, was an important figure in corralling his period into these distinctive narratives of progress. He imposed an influential template of progressive plots on time. Smiles asserted that the future was (or could be) the site of gain, particularly on offer to a hard-working aspirant who was devoted to the notion that tomorrow should be better than yesterday. Smiles told his readership eye-catching stories of looking ahead. He wrote of the rewards of personal labor, the blessings of improving oneself, and the great value of "getting on" in life by one's own effort. In his celebrated but now almost unreadable manual, *Self-Help with Illustrations of Conduct and Perseverance* (1859), Smiles declared that "self-help" was the best agent for the improvement of middle-class futures. And so, of course, was perseverance. Framing this idea, Smiles unknowingly gave a name, "self-help," to a whole generation of later texts: how to be confident; how to be happy; how to succeed in business; how not to worry.

Samuel Smiles announced as a certainty that "honorable advancement in life" was the aim for all energetic and respectable men, and their own actions could achieve it. The idea of "advancement" was to render human life a self-propelled story of change; to suggest that what mattered was moving away by our own effort from who and where we were, or had been, into a future state that was better and different. It is a version of a secular idea of conversion: St. Augustine's experience is turned into a model of how to make money and alter one's class position. The idea of individual advancement privileged the unturned pages of a diary. And no one could assist us like we could ourselves. The self-progressing person, the man with his own eye on the future, was the new desirable subjectivity of the modern middle class.

Cultural forms belong within, but are not merely determined by, the time that invented them. Art is not a reflection of its historical moment but can, of course, have an intimate and creative relationship with that moment, its values and assumptions. A work of literature is, apart from anything else, a way of thinking, a practice of attention, which is in imaginative negotiation—a conversation and sometimes an argument—with the age in which it was made. And on the topic of European modernity's transformed relationship with time cultural critics, as well as imaginative writers, thought hard.

As the nineteenth century grappled with the allure as well as the peril of regarding unknown futures, countercultural voices reminded the age of something of what it was jeopardizing in ditching the potential virtues and values of the inherited past. As the nineteenth century is the period that experiences the invention of modernity as an ambition for the fashionable and the fresh, so it is also the period that peculiarly ruminated on what was at stake in losing the past. If modernity is Protestant in the sense that it envisages the breaking of history's icons as a requirement for progress, there is still, in the nineteenth century, a strand of figuratively (though rarely actually) Catholic assessment of the damage done by the abolition of history's remains. Many of these considerations were local—they concerned only particular versions of the past, particular forms of consuetude and practices of the body. But in anxieties about what new machinery did to men, what value there was in fashioning things by hand, and what principles there were in building in historical styles, were glimpses of matters more generally involved in the modern world's composite neglect of history. The nineteenth-century critics of modernity's forgetfulness had their own personal interests and specialisms, as well as their own biases. But they were, taken as a whole, significant as writers and thinkers against the grain of a culture aspiring toward tomorrow.

The British poet, designer, and utopian William Morris (1834–96) was sure, to take an example, that the past could be, and ought to be, touched. He was no deep thinker, yet his ideas are suggestive. Morris thought that it was by objects that his century could retain something of the vitality of what had once been, of the old ways. Aspiring to champion a return to "traditional" crafts and hand labor in the manufacture of household furnishings and interior design, William Morris proposed how his generation could literally keep hold of (an aspect of) history. The Arts and Crafts Movement, the emergence of which was partly his responsibility, privileged manual work against the trends of the contemporary machine age. Modernity had downgraded manual work: Morris aspired to recuperate it as his own rebuff to modernity's forgetting. The "old-fashioned" manufacturing techniques of preindustrial years were exactly those to resist contemporary absorption with the shifting chimera of fashions. Hand working, Morris asserted, was a way of saving lives. Actual lives, perhaps—but more particularly mental ones. That was because hand labor did not transform people into mindless equipment fabricating, as the modern world often required, valueless commodities for a marketplace enthralled with the new.

The "great achievement of the nineteenth century," William Morris's utopian *News from Nowhere* (1890) declared, "was the making of machines which were wonders of invention, skill, and patience, and which were used for the production of measureless quantities of worthless make-shifts." The notion of a "make-shift" captures adroitly modernity's fascination with purchasing that which must be replaced, of shopping as a Sisyphean task of buying what will always need to be bought again. Breaking from this pattern and undoing the century's new industrial practices in order to restore medieval ways was not a thorough program for changing the priorities of the modern. But the important point was diagnostic. Morris perceived modernity's attention to the new as a risky amnesia, the fracturing of a connection with history at a cost to the mental life and, as we would say, the "well-being" of laboring men and women. He provoked thought not only about reconnecting the modern world to a particular form of working. He asked his readers to understand how the revival of former habits of labor put men and women back in touch with themselves. Hand weaving, block printing, simpler practices of joinery without machine-made components: each was, for Morris, a recuperative form of endeavor that did not dissociate people from their own identities.

Few spoke more amply about the disjunctures in humanity's relationship with time brought by modernity than the English-Scottish art and social critic John Ruskin (1819–1900). His High Tory politics could not have been further from Morris's utopian socialism. Yet both

men, despite the conflict of their politics, were theorists of forgetting
and its perils. Ruskin was permanently interested in what he saw as
the teaching of the past. He thought that, in all branches of human
culture, disassociation from history's achievements was injurious to
creativity, morality, and mental as well as national security. Such disassociation was, for both an individual and his or her society, dangerous, as Ruskin conceived it, to matters of mind and spirit. Alongside
Morris's attraction to the practices and substances of history, Ruskin
pondered the way in which objects, hard and tangible things, remembered. He conceptualized memories on which you could place your
hands, and all such memories implied a resistance to the modern
preference for what was yet to happen.

Like Morris, Ruskin reflected on how it was possible to put men
and women back in touch with history and themselves. He was an
eloquent admirer of sites of memory—the *lieux de mémoire*—and
an articulate advocate of the notion that particular historical locations challenged the forward motion of time by retaining bonds
with earlier lives and values. These values were not axiomatically
good. But Ruskin was prepared to accept that they *could* be good.
Ruskin wanted men and women of the nineteenth century to be
able to live in the company of history that instructed and pleased.
His emblem here was the way, literally, the citizens of medieval
Siena, Venice, and Verona had once existed in civic spaces containing the external tombs of men and women deserving of reverence.
Inviting his readers to attend to the illumination provided by the
finest achievements of individuals and institutions from the past,
Ruskin described the folly of dismantling them, ignoring them, or
forgetting them. Great things, he meant, and great deeds, should
not slip from mind.

In *The Stones of Venice* (1851–3), the most significant book in
English in the nineteenth century on Venetian architecture, Ruskin

discerned in the history of the Sea City's rise and fall an exemplary, though now much contested, account of a city state as it emerged into the modern age. *The Stones* was the narrative of a once admirable community that had, at the beginning of the Renaissance, abandoned its ancestral faith in God in favor of believing in man. Venice had, in another sense, given up the past in preference for the future. The city, as Ruskin saw it, threw out her inheritance. Venice, in Ruskin's scheme, had accordingly succumbed to decadence and death. Here was a history that modern Great Britain—a mercantile power similarly dependent on sea-brought trade—might, Ruskin said, wisely recall. Remembering a culture that remembered its own values and the legacy of its past was potentially recuperative for a hectic modernity intent only on what was new.

It was in ecclesiastical and domestic buildings, in northern Italy and elsewhere, that Ruskin especially perceived his own version of the vitality of the best of the past. Gothic architecture was an outward sign for Ruskin, as for other Gothic Revivalists in the same period, of a refreshed connection with the reverence and respect of medieval Catholic Europe (there was some theological difficulty here for Ruskin who was an Evangelical Protestant at the beginning of his life but fundamentally Catholic in his regard for the achievements of the past). He perceived in Gothic buildings a still-visible continuum with ancestral ways of being, doing, and believing. This was his own version of, his own contribution to, a more general resistance to forgetting; a celebration of what earlier generations had bequeathed to their descendants. In a revival of such architecture, Ruskin observed, there would be an external indication of the spiritual and moral rejuvenation of the nineteenth century achieved by remembering rather than hoping. The past would come alive in bricks and mortar, and the mind and heart would be renewed. Looking backward through buildings to histories he thought the modern world losing, Ruskin found in the local and specific sphere of architecture what had nobly been achieved long ago the best prospects for what should now happen.

Ruskin was a writer seeking in his own distinctive fields to resist the futures-oriented world in which he believed he lived. Given to melancholy, he was peculiarly drawn to mourning breaks with the past: lost parents, lost places, lost loves. Ruskin was an innocent and elegiac witness to the discarding of history, not in buildings only but also in his own life, just as much as he was a celebrator of that which clung on despite the focusing of European capitalism on tomorrow. Through the remaining testimony of architecture, the intentions and priorities of ancestral builders were still legible, Ruskin thought. Amid a culture turning its back on history, here was a small but important way of valuing what had once been achieved. Looking, for instance, at partially surviving medieval carvings in the central gate of the northern French city of Rouen, Ruskin declared in *The Seven Lamps of Architecture* (1849), another celebration of the Gothic buildings of Northern Europe, that we had not wholly lost the ideas of the nearly forgotten men who had carved them. "All else for which the builders sacrificed," Ruskin observed, seeing the traces of a once dignified building,

> has passed away—all their living interests, and aims, and achievements. We know not for what they laboured, and we see no evidence of their reward. Victory, wealth, authority, happiness—all have departed, though bought by many a bitter sacrifice. But of them, and their life, and their toil upon the earth, one reward, one evidence, is left to us in those gray heaps of deep-wrought stone. They have taken with them to the grave their powers, their honors, and their errors; but they have left us their adoration.

From any such survivals of once admirable achievements, the nineteenth century could assure itself, Ruskin pointed out, that the masons who fashioned the originals had left something of their meaning, their priorities and affections, behind. Here was a legacy of blessing. And it was worth understanding, worth cherishing, despite the modern haste to forget, to look away—and to pull the old down.

There was, Ruskin said as a young man, a kind of immortality in peerless historical structures. "There is no such thing as *forgetting* possible to the mind," the Romantic period critic and opium addict, Thomas De Quincey (1785–1859), had once observed: "a thousand accidents may, and will interpose a veil between our present consciousness and the secret inscriptions on the mind; accidents of the same sort will also rend away this veil; but alike, whether veiled or unveiled, the inscription remains forever." Ruskin could never have said anything like that. But he might have appreciated De Quincey's architectural term "inscription" because Ruskin comprehended the durable nature of memory partly in terms of stone.

The protests of buildings against the perceived intellectual and emotional directions of the age were, Ruskin suggested, unique. Such architecture was, physically, a form of remembrance in bricks, arches, buttresses, and carvings. "[There] are but two strong conquerors of the forgetfulness of men," Ruskin observed in *The Seven Lamps*: "Poetry and Architecture; and the latter in some sort includes the former, and is mightier in its reality." When such structures, communicating and preserving their historical reality together with fragments of their founders' intentions, were destroyed, history's remaining meanings passed from the possession of us all.

Books were less liable to such loss. No one, at any rate, tries to restore them in quite the same way as a crumbling or perhaps merely no longer fashionable building. And libraries, for Ruskin, were repositories of cultural memory, enduring forms of teaching, too. His energy in articulating a theory of books as resistant to the urge of modernity was part of his same impulse to save rather than discard, to examine rather than erase. And, where books were concerned, Ruskin's impulse produced, surprisingly, a concept of reading as a strange kind of séance. Ruskin was interested in, and emotionally dependent for a while on, real séances. But the figurative version found in any good library was neither personal nor improbable. History's ghosts were the voices of the dead that still persisted in speaking their minds through published pages. In the touch of hard objects like gates and gables, Ruskin declared, the past was sensible. But it was actually audible, like a living voice, in words printed on paper. Recollecting the testimony of wise books—the "great concourse of the Dead," Ruskin called them in 1864—was to be in touch with those who taught us "not merely to know from them what is True, but chiefly to feel with them what is just." Reading intelligently was to preserve contact with, to listen afresh to, histories that might instruct. Books sent a metaphorical telegram not across space but time.

Modernity produced its own critics, however much they were concerned with localized or particularized areas of life, like building or wallpaper. Turning away from history, modernity invited protest in whatever way was possible from those who thought, across different aspects of human endeavor, that tomorrow was not always, or certainly not self-evidently, the only location of the good, the wise, or the just. And yet, paradoxically, the idea of the future as the place of improvement, as implicitly preferable to the past, seeped into the retelling of history itself during that same century. The principles of the contemporary world are hard to escape. Modernity's rejection of the historical became, metamorphosed, an odd assumption of historians themselves in the period in which modernity was being fashioned. Narrating the past emerged in the nineteenth century, counterintuitively, as a future-oriented business: it was at once about remembering but also about expecting.

In strands of nineteenth-century thinking, history and the idea of "what was to come" merged. It was a distinctive feature of intellectual life and its comprehension of time. The result was the influential concept, at least in the actual business of narrating the past, of what has become known as "Whig History." Here, as the Canadian liberal economist John Kenneth Galbraith (1908–2006) might have said, were ideas "marvelously in the service of circumstance." "Whig History" is the name for a concept in historiography—ideas about how history are conceived and relayed, about how history itself is formulated—which privileged improvement; which regarded the past as an upward trajectory reaching toward where we are now and, implicitly, where we will be tomorrow. Ruskin and Morris envisaged various forms of return to what had gone before as preferable—spiritually, intellectually, aesthetically—to the present. But Whig historians—most prominently at first Lord Macaulay (1800–59)—found primarily in the annals of the past a narrative that, strange to say, privileged what happened next. They did so because the "next" in historiographical terms was, as the Whigs perceived it, better than what had occurred previously. These were writers of growth narratives; of history as goal orientated.

Such historiography internalized a cultural preference for looking ahead by transforming the past into something best understood as a sequence of events always moving toward the (apparent) apex of the present (and beyond). Sir Herbert Butterfield (1900–79), Regius Professor of History and Vice-Chancellor of the University of Cambridge, produced a classic formulation of this understanding of the past in *The Whig Interpretation of History* (1931). He spoke of Whig historians as those with a readiness "to praise revolutions provided they have been successful, to emphasize certain principles of progress in the past and to produce a story which is the ratification if not the glorification of the present." Merge the task of examining what had happened together with modernity's absorption with what will occur: the result for the Whig historians was an account of the past that was best comprehended forward.

The future-facing nature of such history, so different from the impulses of Ruskin, Thomas Carlyle (1795–1881), Morris, or the Gothic Revival architect A. W. N. Pugin (1812–52), was a powerful as well as an influential conception of how to relate the present to what had already happened. We are still negotiating with it. When modern journalists or contemporary historians declare that the purpose of studying the past today is to discover what errors to avoid in the future, they are dimly echoing the principles of the Whigs. They are thinking of upward movement, of the next-as-potentially-better. Yet this notion of historical narrative as developmental, as moving toward achievement, was not confined to the literal task of narrating history. It leaked into, as it was shaped by, cultural forms that had, on the surface, different priorities.

Whig history's assumptions—the assumptions of modernity itself—lie under the principal literary form of the nineteenth century. The century began in literary terms with the Romantic period poets—Byron, Coleridge, Keats, Shelley, Wordsworth—and poetry did not die after them. Victorian period verse—Matthew Arnold, the Brownings, George Meredith, the Rossettis, Algernon Charles Swinburne, Alfred Tennyson—was not weak. But the crown of literature passed from the poets nevertheless. The novel, in both realist and sensation modes, established itself in this century as the most popular and capacious form of literary expression. Poetic reflection gave way to narrative (though some poets, Tennyson and Elizabeth Barrett Browning among them, fought back with narrative poetry), to psychological analysis, to character rather than themes, to plot rather than the peculiarity of moments, to prose rather than the harmonious ordering of poetic line. And if nineteenth-century verse was often detached from modern or public topics—more interior than exterior—the realist novel of the nineteenth century was immersed in them. The genre proved to be ideal for the imaginative consideration of major cultural issues. But it is not the capacity of the nineteenth-century novel to examine the subject matter of modernity, including, for instance, employment, poverty, sexual impropriety, or financial fraud, which is its only intimate connection with the age. Another relationship between fiction and cultural ideas is found in the fact that the nineteenth-century novel is unmistakably the product of a period intrigued by the sensations of what comes next.

The pleasures of the nineteenth-century novel lie in development, in tension, in the unraveling of mysteries, and in long-worked-for climax. This kind of fiction is a practice of writing in which the reader turns the pages because the experience of reading is intently in forward-motion, and sometimes thrillingly so. We comprehend, in contact with these texts, that the fascination with the "next" is driving us on, generating an appetite for traveling in pages toward an unknown region. Futurity in such narratives is where we will find—so we are promised—explanations, satisfactions, and conclusions. Modernity's primary assumptions about the priority of what we do not know in the days and months to come are here, with distinctive success and cultural visibility, plotted in imaginative worlds.

Charles Dickens (1812–70), the most popular of all the major post-Romantic nineteenth-century novelists, began his career in the eighteenth-century manner. He wrote journalistic sketches that were collected together as picaresque. *The Pickwick Papers* (1836)—its full title is *The Posthumous Papers of the Pickwick Club, Containing a Faithful Record of the Perambulations, Perils, Travels, Adventures and Sporting Transactions of the Corresponding Members*—is his first novel, or at least apparently so. Yet *Pickwick* is not an example of the form in the way the later century would understand. A looped or "perambulatory" sequence of episodes—barely in any sense a series—involving a small group of the same characters, *Pickwick* has the charm of the compendium, the society "papers" it pretends to represent. Its pleasures are different from those of a single coherent story, let alone of an entwined plot with many strands slowly being skeined out, which entices us to turn the pages to find out what happened next. In *Pickwick*, what comes next is important primarily in the sense that the reader hopes the next episode will be as amusing as the previous one. But "what comes next," the turn of events ahead, became for Dickens after *Pickwick*, as the world around him addressed itself to the excitement of tomorrow, the ground of a different kind of fiction. The new novel in Dickens's more mature hands was one that exploited the stimulation of unknown but enticing futures with bravura.

Dickens's best popular successes, then as now, are long mystery narratives. *Bleak House* (1852–3), *Great Expectations* (1860–1), and *Our Mutual Friend* (1864–5) are substantial texts that trace out enigmas that cannot be concisely explained. The connection between Esther and Lady Dedlock in *Bleak House* takes sixty-seven chapters to discover. The mystery of Pip's benefactor's identity in *Great Expectations* sustains much of the volume, and the puzzle of the connection between the opening chapters and the rest sustains all of it. Similarly, the conundrum of whether the missing heir John Harmon is dead or not keeps the reader of *Our Mutual Friend* in suspense in a novel as long as *Bleak House*. And as if to intensify the yearning for the next stage, for an explanation of what is happening, Dickens's pioneering publishing style fortified anticipation and turned it into a new source of profit and pleasure.

Pickwick Papers had been published in installments. That suited *Pickwick*'s compartmentalization. But for Dickens's mature fiction, with his long, complex plots of mystery, the same practice of serialization reemerged as a good medium for increasing the reader's tension, their desire for the future. Dickens's installments, most often, came out once a month. In the case of *Bleak House*, the serialized sections, published as stand-alone pamphlets by the London publisher, Bradbury and Evans, were issued as well as heavily advertised from March 1852 to September 1853. In the last number, readers were gratified with a double installment that finally explained the mysteries in a long-awaited culmination of revelation. Up to this point, purchasers of the 1 shilling installments—and those who read and listened to them—had had to wait, between each publication, for 4 weeks. That was more than enough time to speculate, guess, and wonder—as well, of course, to forget. But those gaps, the rewards of waiting, trained the mind in modernity's general habits, like all serialized forms of publication. Even the ways of publishing a novel, in the age of the novel, were imbricated with the values of a commodity capitalism absorbed by what had not yet happened.

Dickens's mystery plots and his distinctive mode of publication were not the choice of every writer of fiction in the nineteenth century. But, to speak generally, the broad corpus of the novel, including fictions by Anne, Charlotte, and Emily Brontë, Wilkie Collins, George Eliot, Thomas Hardy, Elizabeth Gaskell, and Anthony Trollope, involved a natural captivation with the lure of ongoing, purposeful narrative, even if they did not use serialization. That was the nature, and the pleasure, of suspenseful fiction. Here in multilayered form is literature-as-tension. Here are plots that induce forecasting: of wondering about the next stage, and of trying to reach it by reading. These fictions are, although they have the charm of concluding, tales immersed in an anticipation of reward, predicated on the appeal of uncertain futures.

Whig historiography and the realist and sensation fictions of the nineteenth century breathe the air of anticipation. But a novel could still lament the culture that produced it. Fiction gave to the nineteenth-century author the literary amplitude, the verbal volume, to probe the conditions of modern living and its psychological consequences. If it were a forward-facing genre, a novel could still be backward looking. Searching out, and memorializing, the drift of the modern away from remembering, the unanchoring of the contemporary from its connection to history, was not by any means excluded as a topic from some of the period's most substantial fictions. Here, as the English literary critic John Bayley (1925–2015) might have said, was a peculiar use of division. Ruskin and Morris hoped the citizens of modernity could lay their hands on the hard substances of the past. George Eliot (1819–80), author of some of the most philosophical novels of Victorian England, invited her readers to experience history's loss through sympathetic acceptance, through imaginatively *feeling* the pain, of the dispossession of others.

Eliot, as it happens, was interested more generally in the stories of the nearly forgotten. In the age that was beginning to entice its citizens to overlook the past, she was imaginatively attracted to what was overlooked in what she framed as customary representations of that past. In *Middlemarch: A Study in Provincial Life* (1871–2), Eliot's most celebrated realist novel, she pondered the events of unregarded, unrewarded lives. Her imagination conjured existences hidden away in unfashionable parts of the countryside—she is a novelist of middle and marginal places not of centers and cities—in seemingly unremarkable times. There have been many unheard-of St. Theresas, Eliot's narrator observes in *Middlemarch*, thinking of the Spanish saint, Theresa of Ávila (1515–82). These women of large minds and broad sympathies have not merely been forgotten but, she says, were hardly ever known. There have been many, Eliot continues in the "Prelude" to *Middlemarch*, "who found for themselves no epic life wherein there was a constant unfolding of far-resonant action; perhaps only a life of mistakes, the offspring of a certain spiritual grandeur ill-matched with the meanness of opportunity; perhaps a tragic failure which found no sacred poet and sank unwept into oblivion." But such oblivion is what *Middlemarch* narratively resists, setting itself the challenge of recuperating (though of course inventing) stories of those on the edge. In a contest of fiction with forgetting, Eliot's plot drives us forward. But her eye is on the illusion of the recovery of human pasts nevertheless.

Middlemarch pushed against amnesia. But Eliot had also earlier written on the troubling modern theme of unmooring from history, finding it the starting point for a new form of provincial tragedy. If there is a fictional history that metonymically mourns the narrative I have been relating in general terms about the nineteenth century, it is George Eliot's *The Mill on the Floss,* published in three volumes by the Edinburgh publisher William Blackwood in 1860. And, for Eliot, in another echo of the principal unit of the earliest human communities, it is the family in which continuations are most vividly conceived and narrated. The past, in *The Mill,* is both accessible through and peculiarly vulnerable in blood.

The Mill on the Floss is set in an undated time. All we know is that it is a preindustrial moment at some point after the French Revolutionary Wars and prior to the Great Reform Act of 1832. Eliot sketches a rural environment like something painted by the English artist John Constable (1776–1837), distinguished for his recollections of premodern English countryside in which human beings, the natural world, and the passage of time are in a harmonious relationship. There is no violent dislocation in Constable's most characteristic pieces. Yet the story of *The Mill* is Eliot's meditation on dislocation nevertheless, alert to shifts in modern comprehensions of time even in a novel that does not allow us an exact sense of what the time is. *The Mill* is a rueful narrative that projects a culture's breaking with the past—and all its unfathomable implications—onto the local history of a disappointed young woman in love. It's a personalized past, of course; a past that belongs to individuals more than wider communities, to families rather than cities let alone cultures. But, bringing macrohistory into the living room, bringing the general truth into the imagined particular, Eliot poignantly adumbrates that grander narrative.

The family gathered around Mr. Tulliver's water mill makes memory easy. The past is known more than it is actively recalled here, in Eliot's plot, because it is everywhere and unchanged. Maggie, the novel's heroine, grows up with her mother's history literally beside her. There is no sense of the pastness of history because things continue: traditions, employments, homes, objects, space. Here is the dimmest after-echo of the remotest cultures, the family unit and its traditions that seemingly defined the earliest of human societies, long before Mycenae. The mill has been in Mr. Tulliver's family for generations. And what Maggie understands about her life is prompted, everywhere, by the mnemonics of place. Her mother's sisters—Maggie's aunts—are repositories of the family's values, too, their respectable consciences. They are also literally custodians of the family's possessions: the linen and crockery that belong not to individuals but to an idea. That family is constraining, of course: its values are not generous and its views on education, sexuality, appearance, and authority are heavy. Yet Maggie comes to consciousness in a local world that is in living contact with its own precursors. She is no alien to history and to that extent she is secure. Maggie, as she loses her past, bears the burden of Eliot's perception of what abandonment means.

Maggie's life among continuations, that is to say, does not last. Mr. Tulliver loses a lawsuit that he should never have begun. As a result, he plunges his family into debt and their property must be sold. Mr. Tulliver has wrought havoc on the present and its connection with domestic histories—and for no good reason. All with which Maggie and her brother Tom have grown up, the marks of their family's continuations, is to be sold. The literal break-up of the household is the tangible emblem of loss in this striking fable of how far, so to speak, modernity was from Mycenae. Perceiving a few of her favorite books, saved in the bailiff's sale from the family's property, Maggie is overcome by the alteration in her relationship with domestic time. It is a key moment in Eliot's lament for the vanishing of the immediacy of memory, inscribed into the experience of a family forced from its home. Here is a sad, local, and feminized version of an Aeneas hoping to rebuild the past who cannot. Maggie is reminded not of what remains but of the immensity of what does not. "O but, Tom," Maggie says,

> her eyes filling with tears, as she rushed up to the table to see what books had been rescued. "Our dear old *Pilgrim's Progress* that you colored with your little paints; and that picture of Pilgrim with a mantle on, looking just like a turtle—O dear!" Maggie went on, half sobbing as she turned over the few books. "I thought we should never part with that while we lived—everything is going away from us—the end of our lives will have nothing in it like the beginning!"

In Maggie's attachment to childhood books is captured grief for change, for the dismantling of an existence that contained "the same sum of dear familiar objects," a family separated from its own history. For commodity capitalism the idea that the end of our lives should have nothing in them like the beginning is success. For George Eliot's Maggie and the dispossession she figures, it is bereavement.

Writing between 1859 and 1860, Eliot was in part remembering her own childhood home in Warwickshire. There is a private poignancy to *The Mill on the Floss*'s elegiac mood because Eliot was obliged, as she planning it, to remember what before she had simply known. Eliot's brother Isaac had been her favorite. But

Isaac—proud, respectable, hard-hearted—had instructed a solicitor to advise his sister that she could have no further contact with her family. This was because Eliot had begun to live with the philosopher and scientific theorist George Henry Lewes (1817–78). She was not married to Lewes, though she wanted to be—a complicated legal problem probably prevented his divorce. It is a painful personal history of sundering obliquely retold in Tom's rejection of Maggie in *The Mill*. But the poignancy of personal alienation is not the only source of the novel's emotional power. Mapping, through the domestic, the outlines not merely of private estrangement but the cultural shift in nothing less than modernity's relationship with the clock, this sorrowful novel speaks obliquely through its story of a nearly forgotten rural life of the ending of continuations in general. Written in a narrative form freshly oxygenated by the age, *The Mill*, offering its cartography of the pains of losing history, is an expressive examination of an imagined young woman who cannot find where home is. The novel makes local and personal a guiding narrative of its day.

3

Contemporary cultures of amnesia

"Yesterday, Today, Tomorrow
No time to sit and wait on what to write
No time to think of what is right
Forget yesterday
Think only of tomorrow"

Leroy Altman, "Yesterday, Today, Tomorrow" (2014)

One of the shared myths of ancient Greece, one of the communal narratives that no one could easily forget, was a conception of the underworld as a location reached by crossing five rivers. The names of the rivers were Acheron (sorrow, woe), Cocytus (lamenting), Phlegethon (fire and fury), and Styx (hate). The fifth river was Lethe: the waters of forgetfulness.

Drinking Lethean currents has passed now into the proverbial—a way of saying that we have completely failed to remember something. But for the ancient Greeks the river was symbolic of part of the psychic journey of loss, the mental narrative of departure. Once this stream had been entered during the journey beyond the grave, memory of past life was washed away. The dead—they are luminously depicted in

John Spencer Stanhope's canvas now in Manchester City Art Gallery called *The Waters of Lethe by the Plains of Elysium* (1880)—were cleansed in their minds as well as their bodies. The deceased were provided with a psychological as well as physical new start, a fresh consciousness awaiting experience rather than ruminating on it. Lethe and its traversing is a version of what would become Purgatory in Catholic Christianity. The souls "moved on in scorching heat to the plain of Forgetfulness," in the words of the Oxford Greek scholar Benjamin Jowett (1817–93), translating Plato's *Republic*, "and rested at evening by the river Unmindful, whose water could not be retained in any vessel; of this they had all to drink a certain quantity—some of them drank more than was required, and he who drank forgot all things." On the edge of the land of shades, these waters were a prophylactic against nostalgia, a way of preventing the departed mourning what and whom they had left behind. In the heart of a memory culture, the idea of Lethe could not have more plainly indicated for the ancient Greeks the difference between the living, with their devotion to the past, and the dead, with their obliviousness of it.

The Lethean languages that lap around every day encourage us, however, to face away from pasts on this side of the grave. Lethe is now, in our forgetful normalities, for both the quick and the dead. And from Lethe arises, in the present, the siren inheritors of the Victorians' increasing involvement with what comes next, with the present moment as the penultimate, with "now" only as a precursor. And, as we are invited to face forward persistently and variously, our pasts, our sense of what had happened before, slips away in the stream of Lethean oblivion more hastily than ever.

The compound experience of contemporary life that extends the work of the nineteenth century in taking us into forgetfulness is indeed—compound. It is technological, financial, psychological, and material. It is about motion and skylines, supermarkets and finance, marketing and management, the seen and the unseen, the touchable and the ineffable. It is, to start somewhere tangible, to do with the simple business of transportation in the contemporary world as a characteristic and necessary habit of city life. Modernity's transformation of modern time began, in the nineteenth century, in the railway station. And it continues to flourish in the world of motion. The technology of contemporary travel, particularly the high-speed train, the advanced motor car, the airplane and spaceship—inheritors of Victorian inventions—continues to determine an individual's understanding of the relationship between space and the clock. But that technology, more extensively for us than for our predecessors in the nineteenth century, generates patches of what can only be called a peculiarly Lethean experience on a frequent or even daily basis.

Men and women learned from the nineteenth century to understand how timetables—a word that obtains its modern sense with the railways in 1838—acculturated them to forgetting. They encouraged travelers to ignore that which had recently happened and to look ahead to the next moment (the next train, the next tram). The modern traveler, covering greater distances at higher speed, knows this more intently. And he or she also comprehends new expanses of time that, now, must largely be forgotten. The British novelist Virginia Woolf (1882–1941), analyzing the relatively new technology of the aircraft in an essay only published after her death, thought there was something energizing about being lifted into the sky: "Everything had changed its values seen from the air," Woolf wrote in "Flying Over London" (1950): "Personality was outside the body, abstract." This was, at least some of the time, a thrilling sensation of modernity, an opportunity for perceiving oneself, as well as the land, differently. But the abstraction from time, as well sometimes from the self, is, otherwise, disorientating. The long-haul flight, for example, is, as the contemporary world knows, a period in a composite way lost, despite

Woolf's enthusiasm for the air. The traveler slips between time zones, unable to realign his or her body's sense of chronology with what the clock actually says (*which* clock should I be using? I wonder, uncertain of the zone I am flying over). Hours cease to have regular meaning. The journey in turn mystifies its relation to time, occurring beyond our normal comprehensions. And, more plainly, the period spent in such roaring metal tubes is rarely productive—a movie, some food, a sleep. Arrival is the moment to put the experience out of mind.

That loss of time is true on a more daily, more modest, basis because of the "commute." The American short story writer and essayist Washington Irving (1783–1859) was a deft evaluator of the practices of mind that city life created. The modern man in town, Irving said in *The Sketch-book of Geoffrey Crayon, Gent* (1819–20), has permanently "a look of hurry and abstraction." He is the embodiment, Irving went on, of a fretful preoccupation with where he is not in time, space, and mind: "Wherever he happens to be, he is on the point of going somewhere else; at the moment he is talking on one subject, his mind is wandering to another[.]" The modern city and its margins, the modern city and its living costs, oblige inhabitation of edges. Here is the territory of actual and, as Irving would have expressed it, mental dis- and relocation.

The urban spaces of contemporary normalities separate men and women from what they do and where they live. The commute, utilizing whichever form of transport, is habitually lost or shadow time, a period to be lived through not in, an experience that's primarily transitionary, like waiting for the kettle to boil. The commute's diurnal recurrence is part of its deadness, too: journeys are the same, undifferentiated except by unexpected delays or strange behavior from fellow travelers, drivers, or passengers. The term "commute" signifies in the penitentiary a reduction in a judicial sentence, a cutting-short of time served and the unexpected extension of freedom. It is bizarrely the same word that also signifies not time freed but lost, not time reduced but time extended in a state of mental detachment that is a distinctive sensation— or *lack* of sensation—generated by the periods that bookend our working days.

Karl Marx (1818–83) and Friedrich Engels (1820–95) remarked in *The Communist Manifesto* (1848), their theatrical and gestural protest against the logic of bourgeois capitalism, that: "The bourgeoisie cannot exist without constantly revolutionizing the instruments of production." The bourgeoisie—the middle classes with property—retained power partly through perpetual busyness. But in the advanced capitalism of the twenty-first century, what is more immediately obvious is an almost constant revolution in technology, including the instruments of communication. It is not so much the relationship with production that is changing at a dizzying pace as the phones. Yet that has, as Marx and Engels would have recognized, consequences on how we perceive our connection with time and space, as well as each other, too.

The Italian Futurist Filippo Tommaso Marinetti (1876–1944) was angrily committed to the abolition of the past in celebration of the pace of modernity. "We stand on the last promontory of the centuries!" he said in his *Manifesto del Futurismo* (1909): "Why should we look back, when what we want is to break down the mysterious doors of the Impossible? Time and Space died yesterday. We already live in the absolute, because we have created eternal, omnipresent speed." He was referring to machines and the rapidity of technological development. He would, no doubt, have regarded contemporary electronic messaging systems, to take but an ordinary example, as avatars of that eternal and supposedly glorious haste. Certainly, the devices we can hold in our hands have dramatically outpaced the nineteenth century as well as Marinetti's age. They have recalibrated humanity's conception of geography in relation to the clock and the exactness of timetabling.

Some forms of time-controlled messaging are so much in conflict with even micropasts that they abolish traces of communications in a few moments. It is possible to send an image through commercial video-messaging software and know that it vanishes forever (supposedly forever, at any rate) after between 1 and 10 seconds. The maximum length of history here is a one-sixth of a minute.

Communication devices, smart phones and tablets, held by fingers are instruments of digital promise. The promise is of the future: the next message, status update, real-time exchange, or e-mail. The devices save lives and they save time. But they speed time up, too, and addict us—the word is not ill-chosen—to a future that's diminished, often enough, to the next few minutes as much as it is localized to where I am, right now. The self-enclosed individual notices little around him or her except the communication of the screen. Time is hurried and space is shrunk. Concentration spans, it has become clear, have reduced among children as well as adults. Researchers at Microsoft ascertained in the spring of 2015 that the average human attention span had become 8 seconds by 2013. That was a reduction of 4 seconds from the average as it was measured in 2000 (12 seconds). Microsoft had also discovered that, in 2013, men and women could concentrate for 1 second less than the amount of time a goldfish can remember. Some individuals can only break their dependence on phones and tablets by disposing of them altogether; by living a newly monkish, pretechnological life. Then, they can hope to outdo the goldfish once again.

Research—and anecdotal daily observation—reveals also that it can, at present, be less than 3 minutes that even a professional, well-educated individual can remain without checking his or her phone to learn what he or she is missing. Reading hard-copy in the presence of a smart phone or tablet can only be done, for those so challenged, in portions of less than 180 seconds. The temptation to see what has happened, to find out whether what we knew has been updated, is hard to throw off. Documents, read on screen or off, are taken in pieces. One of the reasons for reading digital books on a tablet is, perhaps, that notifications of new messages can appear directly on screen, temporarily obstructing the page. The text is automatically interrupted so the reader does not have to break the reading process themselves: the screen does it for them. And as concentration alters, like the time-lapsed pictures from space of melting glaciers, it is easy to become aware how difficult it is to recover the recent history of our own. What *had* I just read?

The faltering of immediate personal history—of reading, writing, talking, or thinking—is conjoined with the expectation of further communication. And the loss of concentration is now seemingly quantifiable by practitioners of the new "interruption science." Interruption scientists are individuals endeavoring to make men and women more "productive" (another futures-driven term) by diminishing what distracts them from work. Consider merely the numbers of notifications that appear on a regular wifi-enabled screen as indicative of both how concentration is destabilized and the short-term future made a focus. Notifications include those for SMS, voice mail, e-mail, social media, paging messages, RSS, and app or operating software updates. We might wait for these messages and we might expect them. But they still distract us when they arrive. "Researchers in the new field of interruption science," notes Pico Iyer in his countercultural *The Art of Stillness: Adventures in Going Nowhere* (2014), "have found that it takes an average of twenty-five minutes to recover from a phone call. Yet such interruptions [for some office workers] come every eleven minutes—which means we're never caught up with our lives. And the more facts come streaming in on us, the less time

we have to process any one of them." The future under such conditions becomes the temporal place where, first, an individual expects
to receive more information (to be "updated"). And it also becomes,
second, the temporal location where he or she aspires to find enough
time to figure out what that updated information means. The future
is, in this respect, both collapsed and postponed.

Lethe promised the Greeks a kind of sleep. And sleep is a blessing.
Dozing off is hard to resist—and so are the mental habits fostered
by ordinary work in front of computers. Even getting started is sur-
rounded by problems of remembering. There are many passwords to
retain. The more unguessable the secret code, the harder it must be to
recollect. What is necessary for security is, by definition, what does
not easily stay in mind. I search Google for "forgotten your password?"
There are, today, 190 million results. That is one site or hit for nearly
two-thirds of the population of the United States or over a quarter of
the population of Europe. Access protocols to websites change frequently, which makes forgetting necessary as well as annoying. Being
prepared to cast into oblivion what I had learned about using website
x or database *y* becomes a condition of a computerized world. That
is because each system (e-mail, a ticket-buying app, a supermarket
delivery service) necessitates knowledge of in-house procedures. Yet
it is only knowledge for a while. What is comprehended is required
but for a short time. The sands shift, the cyber-world alters and trans-
forms neither with our consent nor our control. What we retain today
about this protocol or that screen layout, this way of entering data or
that way of retrieving it, is not what we will need to recall when a new
version, a new upgrade, or a transition to a rival system, occurs. The
internal landscape of these things is in Lucretian change: "verily | In
constant flux do all things stream," the first-century BC Roman poet
says, accidentally sounding as if he is talking about video feeds.

The digital age, successors to the Victorians' achievements, grooms minds to wait impatiently just as it engages with protean uses, and forms, of forgetting. But there is a larger context. The channels of our lives through which the tributaries of Lethe run are deep. Take, for instance, the workplace assumptions that modern men and women are invited to adopt, together with their businesses, which send them further into the lands of (deferred) futures. Here, "what-is-to-come" is, as it was for Samuel Smiles, the envisaged time of improvement. Time is registered as passing but framed as incremental: on today's results, businesses need to build. History's record needs to be known only to be exceeded. The visual representations of this are self-evident. Graphs are encouraging only if they project a rising line; if they reach out into time unknown with the earnest of upward movement. No longer is the perfect the enemy of the good, as the former United States Secretary of State Henry Kissinger used to say. It is the motionless.

For us, remarks the British psychoanalyst Adam Phillips in *Missing Out: In Praise of the Unlived Life* (2012), it has become "the enduring project of our modern cultures of redemption—cultures committed above all to science and progress—to create societies in which people can realize their potential, in which "growth" and "productivity" and "opportunity" are the watchwords (it is essential to the myth of potential that scarcity is scarcely mentioned: and growth is always possible and expected)." Economic growth is a ubiquitous goal. It has established itself as an indicator of a nation's, as well as a single business's, value and purpose, challenged only by wayward individuals whose careers are curtailed, and sometimes ended, by resistance, or even sometimes simply by questioning. This is part, as *Missing Out* agrees, of modern capitalism's sustained project that has involved the transformation of societies, nations, peoples, and cultures into "economies." Growth has become the enduring idea concerning that which is expected to endure: expansion, increase, gain.

Investments that are expected to rise in value and business plans that spell out strategies for future growth—the "action plan" that marks the ways in which those futures will be made to yield—are the commonplace documents of advanced bureaucratic modernity. They are the newest versions, it may be, of the old prophecy; the contemporary successors of what, for the Victorians, the railway time-tables signified. They are where Delphi has gone in the new financial dispensation of future-thinking. These plans are certainly the most daring of contemporary statements that aspire, at least theoretically, to make the future stand and deliver. And if Apollo's Delphic pronouncements were sometimes cryptic, these modern documents of plans and strategies are always to a point fictive. Such plans are buried narratives of supposition grown from facts, guessed suspense plots grounded in data, wagers into the unknown fashioned as aspirations that are purportedly "risk-proofed" (a term that is so recent it has yet to make it into *OED*). These plans invoke a future that allegedly can be bridled, accomplishing a secular transformation of heavenly paradise into earthly gain. Such plans look forward not to what we deserve but what we can organize for ourselves in, to use that ubiquitous cliché of the marketplace, an "increasingly competitive environment." Business futures are seemingly map-able, partly through the so-called scientific models of human economic activity (if we do x, the market will respond y) and partly through the more general confidence that plans themselves have authority, that they are a "route map" to somewhere we have, and possibly want, to go.

Business plans hail the future as that which is apparently controllable so long as all involved participate in the assumption of that control (or at least hide any doubts about it from public view and certainly from a prospective financial backer). Those plans are a portion of the archive of documentation that orients us toward the beyond in ways that suggest, though cannot confirm, that good is on its way, that increase will be upon us presently. Prosperity or security will be obtained, such documents propose, through careful administration, judicious action, and managed gambles on the turn of the next few days, weeks, or months. "[Remember] that your business plan will have any chance of winning the backing it merits if it is coherent, consistent and credible," says Vaughan Evans in *The FT Essential Guide to Writing a Business Plan* (2016), speaking the commonplace language of futures, of the managed gamble in the hope of a "win." But, he adds, "you need to get all your ducks in a row." It is curious how the language of new futures relies on old clichés: the past keeps coming back.

The future, in the context of the plan, is the harbinger of benefit; the subjunctive is a case that looks forward to success. The blurb for Alexander Osterwalder and Yves Pigneur's *Business Model Generation* (2010) puts that plainly. This, we read, "is a handbook for visionaries, game changers, and challengers striving to defy outmoded business models and design tomorrow's enterprises": the future not the "outmoded" past; prophecy not the present. The visionaries are not the exponents of the old but those who can see the profits of the yet-to-come. "So yes," says the British writer Olivia Laing pensively in *To the River: A Journey Beneath the Surface* (2011), her beautiful book that traces a walk along the River Ouse in which Virginia Woolf drowned: "I understand why the island of the sirens is piled high with bodies. If any one of us knew what the future held, I think we too would sit there, petrified, until the hide rotted from our bones." That is a dim echo of a Homeric view, I suppose, deprived of any faith in the capacity of the gods to sort things out or provide us with a future worth waiting for (*To the River* is sternly atheistic). But Laing's trepidation, her acknowledgment of *terra incognita*'s terrors, is not the authorized view of our current habitation. Where we are, the sirens are supposed to be followed.

As institutions and corporations develop what are hailed as "strategies" to deal with the future—a term that derives from the ancient Greek στρατηγία (*strategia*), the name for a military general—so do individuals. The vocabularies of business planning have also become those of self-management and of how others manage us. "Annual appraisal" cohabits workplace vocabularies along with, for instance, "targets," "performance criteria," "job descriptions," and "workload models" ("appraisal," when it means an assessment of someone's performance at work, dates to 1915; "workload" to 1899). All these formulations have their attention on what should be done next and how supposedly to optimize it. These documents, this cluster of specialized terminology that has become modernity's *lingua franca*, concern how individuals should behave primarily in the future and what they should be aiming at in the (usually) short term. Such assumptions are nowhere plainer than in the workplace (and "workplace" itself is a term that is part of the modern geography of forgetting because it invites us to separate portions of our lives depending on the time of day). The most familiar of contemporary documents of an allegedly managed futurity belong in our roles as "employees" (a word that comes into being in 1814). That is to say, they belong with the "personal development plan."

The discourse of "personal development" and all the literal forms and signatures involved in its documentary creation sheers off the "employee" from the supposedly "private" person by redefining "personal." In a sense, we are asked to forget what we are like back at home, and also invited to assume that there is a split within us, a bifurcated self that is one person at work and another away from it, like Wemmick in Dickens's *Great Expectations*. The personal, in the place of labor, is now constructed as primarily the possession of others. The "personal development plan" hails the fact that the personal is now, seemingly, that which is to be shaped by the needs of those in charge—known and unknown. The successful operation of these forms is predicated on an assumption about human nature's ability to self-direct and to transform, to an extent, at will. The principal assumption remains, coherently with the shape of a culture of forgetting, simply that the unknown times ahead are those on which we should concentrate because, carefully managed, they can be made serviceable—or, rather, *we* can be made *more* serviceable. Worry, it might be, the American cultural historian Rebecca Solnit says in *A Field Guide to Getting Lost* (2005), "is a way to pretend that you have knowledge or control over what you don't—and it surprises me, even in myself, how much we prefer ugly scenarios to the pure unknown." But the documents of personal development swear us to a form of antiworry (even if they actually make us worry more since they are bound up with the hyperevaluated world of modern employment practices). The personal development plans assure us, or at least seem to, that we need not choose between Solnit's ugly scenarios and the pure unknown in aspiring to take control over what we do not yet comprehend. Personal development is inscribed with a putatively reassuring conviction that we can work sensibly toward desirable outcomes, and desirable changes, planning our ways to our own (though often enough, someone else's) gain.

"Development" came into the English language as a term referring to the gradual unfolding, or "fuller disclosure," as *OED* says, of a planned scheme, like the plot of a novel or, solemnly, God's will for humankind. "Developed" was, in turn, a past tense synonym for "realized," as in "the original idea has been realized." But it now refers at its rawest level to a business's attempts to encourage, if not require, an employee to "align" themselves with that business's interests in the months to come, the months of the "planning period." Our futures, with an unvarnished literalness, have passed into the custody of corporations and institutions. The plan, at its most basic, is not ours but theirs.

Is there an end point to, an apex of, the "personal development plan" and what it culturally implies? (When I say "apex" I might mean "nadir.") One unexpectedly positive way of looking at these nearly ubiquitous documents and their cultural implications about time is, oddly enough, to welcome them, somewhat counterintuitively, as modest protests *against* the passage of days. These quotidian forms, which are both of little and of exceptional importance in working lives, are at least benignly conceivable as a faint objection to modern ideas of time in the sense that they assume a career, that concept bounded by the status of being an "employee," does not slow down and does not obviously adjust to bodily age (except at the point of retirement). They assume that there is not a moment in which any of us will cease to "develop" or "move forward." They are, to this extent, welcome for the reason that they do not discriminate against the old. And that is a surprise.

The Judeo-Christian God is always an old man. He is the Ancient of Days—the name for Jehovah in the Book of Daniel. With age was obviously, for ancient Judaism and its Christian inheritors, where wisdom lay. In the Pentateuch, God frankly demands respect for the ripened as well as for Himself. "Thou shalt rise up before the hoary head," says Leviticus 19:32, "and honor the face of the old man, and fear thy God." Elihu, in Job 32, waits to speak after those who "were elder than he" (32:4). He must be silent until it is his turn to venture an opinion before reverend personages. Elihu is obeying the injunctions of Leviticus. "Days should speak," he says in Job 32:7, "and multitude of years should teach wisdom." Rather than rendering those rich in years outmoded, or categorizing them with clichés as "the old guard" or the "conservatives," these ancient texts provide us with a glimpse of a remote culture that recognized in older people, if only potentially, a collective wisdom worth at least listening to.

The modern world's way of dealing with age—setting the personal development plan aside—seems almost wholly counter to this. Modernity either surrounds human aging with negatives (to which I will return) or pretends that age is not happening (and that might be the negative way of regarding the fact "personal development plans" are largely innocent of how old we are). The market proliferates images of the young so that even those selected to appear in visual advertisements for care homes, stair-lifts, and will-writing services are suspiciously youthful. We rarely find substantively or substantially interrogated the assumption that youth will be the best source of energy and fresh ideas for the future. When Nestor responds to Diomedes, a warrior second only in distinction among the Greeks to Achilles, in Book 9 of the *Iliad*, his words are not ours. Nestor is respectful of his comrade-in-arms, though Nestor is older: "Son of Tydeus," he says, "above all men are you mighty in battle, and in council are the best among all those of your own age." But Nestor swiftly invokes his culture's assumption that age confers a greater authority than youth, though never an infallible one, and that therefore he may assume (though not abuse) his privilege of years: "But come," Nestor continues, "I who claim to be older than you will speak out and will declare all; nor will any man scorn my words, not even Lord Agamemnon." Age gives gravity and weight to words—or at least must first of all be assumed to do so.

For us, it is the other way around. A company, a charity, a tea shop, or a church: each can be peculiarly sanguine about new blood. The hope for youth as the agent of profitable alteration is the inscription of a deeper desire for the new, for the next, on the bodies of the young. This is itself a practice of forgetting, a turning away from yesterday as a drag-line on progress. Sometimes literally the memories of the old are held up in the workplace only to be discounted. "We tried this before and it didn't work" can easily be made to sound, by those disposed to privilege the newness of the new, like a refusal rather than an effort to be helpful, a block rather than an attempt to avoid failure. In the young, we might now find more readiness to comply, more "appetite" to conform to what will obtain promotion and prospects. So in turn contemporary culture celebrates, and reclassifies, a lack of experience as a welcome new start that is unfreighted by the heavy burden of a past that will not get us where we supposedly want to be.

Modern capitalism has its own uses for temporal unknowns, for postponed gratifications. But, more generally, modern economic competition simply celebrates the new—or at least the supposedly new, the "described-as-new"—as the primary agent of such improvement. Regarding the future as the scene of profit, modern capitalism describes innovation as a peculiar lever of advancement at personal, corporate, and even, dizzyingly, "global" levels. As capitalism focuses on cloudy times ahead, it encourages men and women to assume that the way to obtain mastery over those times is, in part, by invention. Flitting through the convictions of contemporary economic ideas about future prosperity is a pale ghost, a newly financialized wraith, of the Romantic Genius.

That Genius was the Original Man (it usually *is* a man) possessed of, or possessed by, special powers. With them, he worked a form of revolution. Napoleon Bonaparte is the political avatar of this; Faust, as Goethe proposed, the deeply ambiguous intellectual one. Entrepreneurship, the badge of the new visionary today, is a modern equivalent of Samuel Smile's "self-helping" laborer too. The term "entrepreneur" describes—is at least intended to describe—the person who sets out to obtain control of his or her own future by being different. He is the individual, the essential Smilesian self-made man, recast for the present. He achieves what no one, supposedly, had thought of, or brought off, before. He is an inventor and, often enough, one whose creativity is praised because he has typically bypassed the formal structures of education and/or belongs in an unprivileged class position. He is inexplicably gifted like his Romantic period predecessors and those gifts are presented in popular culture as a sign of special favor and of more than ordinary luck that has been allegedly self-created (entrepreneurs are given to saying that a man or a woman "creates their own luck").

Being an entrepreneur initially meant, as *OED* puts it, the same as being an impresario. That is, simply, "one who 'gets up' entertainments, *esp.* musical performances." He was a showman and a manager of shows. So the entrepreneur is now, though usually in a different sense. The entrepreneur manages with flair, and sometimes with brusque laddishness, the theatrical performance of his own self. He provides a seductive narrative, to politicians, journalists, and aspirants, of how it is possible to put reins on the future, to turn one's own life into a rising graph of material gain. He is a man who does not drag his feet, even if that actually means he is a gambler who is unusually fortunate. Doing things differently, inventing processes or commodities, championing undeveloped services or systems, audaciously speculating in ways that will work out: the entrepreneur is the new hero of our time, the new hero of the new. He is a living embodiment of another framing term of the modern eagerness for futures: opportunity.

To believe in the entrepreneur is to have faith in the capacity of an individual to generate prosperity for a company while creating extensive private capital for himself. Such faith is a reprise of the old reverence for trickle-down, that economic theory that is caught between common sense and absurdity ("trickle-down" is well analyzed as "Thing 13" in Ha-Joon Chang's clever dismantling of economic principles in *23 Things They Don't Tell you about Capitalism* (2010)). The key to the entrepreneur's achievement is, among other things, "innovation." And it is worth thinking for a moment where this term sits in relation to domestic, or psychological, values that are less dependent on changing material histories. "Innovation" is part of the modern vocabulary of forgetfulness. But how does it relate to private human desires for the secure?

In family life and in love, "innovation" is not, of course, what we want. The necessity of change and forgetting might be a corporate requirement and, as far as evolutionary theory is concerned, a biological one. But it is discordant, all the same, with a personal hope for something different and less in motion. Usually, we would prefer calm and constancy, not upheaval and alteration. In love and with our families, it is memory that matters, and is more stabilizing, than the hyperventilating appetite for change. Relationships must not become stale or lose their capacity to excite, certainly. We do not wish to be bored by those we love—bored by routine, unchanging views, fixed patterns of mind. But who, except every now and again in bed, would say that it is important in a relationship to "innovate?" Our private desires are for stability and security. But our public personae need, even flamboyantly, to discern in consistency hazard.

Against the grain of a private hope for steadiness, innovation has migrated from the language of commerce into surprising places. The optimism in, and the adherence to, the future appears in so many areas of modern life that it is easy to forget that it's a relatively new companion. It is hard, more generally, not to agree with the English economist John Maynard Keynes (1883–1946) in his hugely influential book *The Economic Consequences of the Peace* (1919) that ideas which are established as orthodoxies have an exceptionally contagious and enduring power beyond their applicability. They outlive their aptness. A new reverence for innovation is evident, for instance, in education, where an outsider might think the tried and trusted had still some continuing appeal. Clive Beck and Clare Kosnik symptomatically regarded the contemporary process of teacher training in the United Kingdom, for example, as needing to be shaken up in their

Innovations in Teacher Education (2006). This provided a manifesto for change under the banner of "innovation" (which did not need a qualifier such as "good" or "sensible"). Isabella Wallace and Leah Kirkman's guide to teaching in turn found, as if another barometer of the age and its commitment to invention rather than the remembered, self-evident value in the "new" (or at least the "described-as-new") inside the classroom itself. These authors published their handbook with an encouraging exclamation mark: *Pimp Your Lesson! Prepare, Innovate, Motivate and Perfect* (2014). The vocabulary of commodity capitalism springs up in schools and universities, colleges and conservatoires—and, for Wallace and Kirkman, it is accompanied by a daunting notion that there is such a thing, somewhere in the future, somewhere in the plan, as "perfect" teaching.

"Innovation" or "innovative" are familiar promotion requirements and a habitual part of the self-description of multiple businesses, institutions, and individuals. Forbes now publishes a list of the year's 100 "most innovative companies;" the search term "'innovative company'" today produced more than half a million results. And the language of the new is tough to escape even for those—historians, archaeologists, musicians, artists, literary critics, lawyers, and modern linguists among them—whose concerns are, in some way or another, with the past. It is revealing, too, how dull, stale, and unprofitable the language of "innovation" is in its public manifestations just as it is revealing how uninnovative it has become to call oneself innovative: "Pimp Your Lesson! ...," "Innovate or die ...," "innovative company." The phrases, like "ducks in a row," are worn down by the number of feet that have paced over them.

Even ministers of the Christian church are expected to innovate (though here as elsewhere that tends to mean doing something similar to others). This is one of the most revealing indicators of the penetration of commercial assumptions about the prestige of an unobtained future into cultural locations where one might assume they would never reach. For the Christian tradition, the unfolding of scriptures and the celebration of the mystery of the Eucharist are ways of remaining in touch with, of literally repeating, practices established in a sacred history. Yet there is also a modern necessity, notably in the United Kingdom, to change matters from how they used to be. It is seemingly a requirement, in the Church of England, to break from that which is "traditional" (solidly in the negative sense) not only in public worship and liturgy, but also, for instance, in the deployment of church space, the distribution of responsibility for ministry, and the raising of both funds and congregational numbers. Ministers, it turns out, need business plans as much as businesses do.

Commodity capitalism extends the nineteenth-century exhilaration with fashion and up-to-dateness into the new marketplaces of the contemporary globalized and computerized world ("globalized" is first recorded in 1929; "computerized" in 1952). Advertisers, through more forms of media than the Victorians comprehended, extend their persuasion of what we ought to possess, of needs we did not realize, of gaps that we did not appreciate we had. Tomorrow becomes that moment when we will be able to satisfy, supposedly, a desire for what today we do not know about, do not own, or cannot yet afford. Here, in terms of psychological patterns, is a resisted version of a romance: a psychological conflict with an erotic impulse that existed long before modernity advised us to look into the future and turn our backs on the past.

Psychoanalysis sometimes figures human life in terms of a joke—implying not that life *is* a joke but that our desires and attitudes, our ways of processing the world, follow a joke's logic. A joke is a narrative directed toward the future. It is an analogy of typical life stories for the psychoanalyst, not a bleak existentialist verity that means everything is so awful that all we can do is laugh. Like a joke is the business of understanding who we are, what we want, and what is wrong with us. A joke is something that we need to "get," as the direction and nature of our lives is something we try to "get" too. It is the humblest and most recognizable form of a narrative that has an end point toward which everything purposefully moves. We listen to a story ("two penguins walk into a bar …") and wait for the punch line. That terminal revelation renders coherent, makes sense of, the brief anecdote that went before it, which most likely was inexplicable or fantastic previously (penguins don't walk into bars …). The punch line is the moment of insight, the dimmest echo of the ancient Greek's ἀναγνώρισις (*anagnorisis*), the temporal point of recognition, and also the place to which the narrative has been traveling without us knowing where it was going in advance.

In the joke is a microcosm of hopes for experience: that we will find the figurative punch line that will cause the past to make sense. The joke, to this extent, creates history—the realization of a pattern in events, and words, of the past. It will show us an intention when we thought there was only expectation; it will reveal a form of logic where there had only been a confused looking ahead during which we wondered how this was all going to work out. The joke, imposing like history a plot on time, is a faint but still credible model of a therapist's work in turning personal stories into a narrative that is moving somewhere. It is a compelling miniature of that analyst's task of reading back from the last line, so to speak, to find the way through, and the direction of, previous experience.

Yet a concern with the multiple shapes of futurity situates us all in a joke, we might say, that has yet to conclude. Contemporary habits of mind are, in these terms, a gag without a last line, a gag without a gag. What we know is that we are waiting for the words that will conclude things, and make sense of them, while not comprehending how far into the joke we are. History is not suddenly made into sense, crystallized into narrative, or purpose, or even visibility. Here is a situation that is as baffling as a joke that is not a joke. The experience of contemporaneity is, to phrase it in these mercurial terms, of waiting to know, and never finding out, what the penguins did in the bar.

The contemporary salutation of that which is yet to come is also, in a different psychological analogy, a love affair without a kiss, a romance without touch. The Victorian novel was the product of a culture orientating itself toward the future even as it, the novel, could eloquently mourn the loss of connections with the past that that embrace of futurity involved. But the pattern of romance, the experience of falling in love, is a human narrative that is not an obvious outcome of a culture looking ahead, however much Karl Marx proposed all human consciousness, desires, and inner lives were constructed by history and its changing material circumstances. Romance, rather, is one of the two areas of life where human beings have, for an indeterminate time, looked ahead for a while anyway (albeit with the hope of not looking ahead soon). To the other—death—there is much to say, but not in this book. Falling in love, the desire for someone else (or at least an idea of someone else), is an experience of hope for tomorrow that is not simply constructed by a futures-driven modernity. When falling in love, a human being is acquainted under pressure with the pleasures and pains of expectation, the fraught anticipation of reward, the chance of touch, intimacy, and sex. Falling in love is to desire, as well as actively to imagine, a future that could, one day, be obtained. It is to regard a point in time when we can, we dream, cease desiring what we do not have and start living in possession of it.

Sigmund Freud tells us that we always seek what we do not want. He remarks that falling in love is persistently an attraction to that which repels. He more generally reminds us that falling in love is not free from history. Falling in love, at however a subliminal level, is a replacement activity that involves either a hope of return to the security of childhood (when that childhood *was* secure) or an effort to compensate for it (when it was not). The loved one in these terms is fungible, a supplement or an exchange with the past, and to that extent falling in love expresses an ambition to arrive somewhere earlier in life, to go backward. But falling in love, despite this pull of history and the chance to repair it, is still to occupy one's mind with an imagined future. Romance lends us a compass that points optimistically to a way in front even if, when we eventually arrive, we discover it different from what we had hoped.

But the romance of the modern world, insofar as romance is a figure of future-longings, is an unconsummated or even unrequited one. Security is postponed: it is suspended before we know of love reciprocated or otherwise. In terms of our contemporary culture's mental direction toward what lies before us, the romance of the present stalls, permanently, before the first touch. We are all, so to phrase it, like the devotee on John Keats's imagined ancient Greek artifact in "Ode on a Grecian Urn" (1819), permanently frozen beside what he wants. "Bold Lover," Keats says of the Attic figure on the vase, "never, never canst thou kiss, | Though winning near the goal." The only way that this situation, so near the "goal" of contacting lips, can alter is if the fragile urn itself is broken. The yearning youth can end his (imagined) pain only when he is turned to powder. The narrative of satisfaction, of finding love reciprocated, is where we are not as Keatsian citizens of a state of perpetual anticipation. We are, instead, situated in a relationship that cannot be consummated.

Part of this is to do with the fact that the desires contemporary culture creates within us for what is to come are those that, even if obtained, will always be replaced by other ones: by new futures, new sets of aspirations, and new plans. There is no reaching the place we're perpetually trying to reach. We are orientated to the minutes, days, and months in a future we cannot know because there is always another future to replace it. We comprehend, too, that fulfilling goals, reaching "targets," raising profits, and satisfying plans will bring us only to where, in our relationship with time, we were before: at the beginning of another plan, prophesying ahead to what is to come next. We still haven't been kissed. Intentions are only followed by other intentions—and an intention, in the form of a plan, can, anyway, be out-of-date within hours of its drafting. In the United Kingdom, this is peculiarly evident in the theatrical drama of the Budget, the Chancellor of the Exchequer's annual statement of what the economy will do next and how it is to be managed. Installed in our expectations is that there will always be a *next* plan—ours or other people's. Plans, determinations to look forward, distribute dissatisfaction with where we are now and aspirations for where we will be soon. They are like joke-shop party candles that can never be blown out. The future is perpetually reenvisaged as the object of new or modified desires at any point that earlier intended futures are obtained, superseded, or forgotten. Here is the paradox of modernity's enchantment with tomorrow: we can't get there.

The Cambridge literary critic Tony Tanner (1935–98) remarked that all novels are about adultery. But, strange to say, so are all plans. They tempt us with new connections and drive ambitions in different paths from the settled and stable as soon as the previous desires have been obtained: as soon as they have been achieved, bypassed, or rendered out-of-date. Plans find in acquisition only the grounds for dissatisfaction, encouraging us each time we reach where we thought we were going (or believe we had reached there) to try to go somewhere else. Those plans, in the world of perpetual futures, situate us faithfully in a situation of infidelity, requiring us to look beyond what we have, or were trying to have, and to realize that, soon, we must desire something else.

In this overdetermined, unfaithful attention to the future, in the multiple orientations of our public and private worlds away from the past and toward tomorrow, capitalism has achieved one of its many strange internal paradoxes. It has rendered us uncertain how to recognize futures that really *are* new. Clustering around our understanding of what is to come is the same aspiration, everywhere, for "innovation." But that aspiration is shaped in an environment in which it has become tricky to assess what actually is innovative, not least when this or that "innovation" is the same as what others are doing simultaneously elsewhere—including saying that they are innovative. Determining the nature of innovation is problematic, too, because it is not at all straightforward, faced with the language of marketing and public relations, to distinguish between what is asserted about a product, commodity, or idea—and what that product, commodity, or idea *is*.

Among the oddest features of psychosis is its ability to possess a human mind in a way that a friend, colleague, or even parent or partner does not recognize for a long time. They might not distinguish it for years. Even a professional therapist can perceive no sign of delusory thinking in their client for substantial periods of time though they intuit that *something* is amiss. A chance remark, a single observation, can reveal that an apparently normal individual has organized their understanding of themselves and the world around them through a psychotic fantasy. And that fantasy might only be glimpsed in a few out-of-the-ordinary words or actions, late in the day. This is like watching M. Night Shyamalan's film *The Sixth Sense* (1999): it takes (many people) a long time to realize the single fact that alters the meaning of everything just seen. "How could it be," the British psychoanalyst Darian Leader reflects in *What Is Madness?* (2011), after quite a few years of witnessing this phenomenon of the delayed awareness of psychosis, "that delusion and everyday life could be so seamlessly woven together? How could one inhabit two apparently different places at the same time as if there were no barrier between them?" Yet, strange to say, we are all acclimatized to the presence of delusion crossing the barriers of "everyday" life more or less—everyday. We are not suffering a mental illness. This is, rather, a condition, an obligation, of modern living. We inhabit a world where daily existence is composed of fictions, hyperbole, and forms of delusion: only here, unlike the psychoanalyst searching for the missing clue of the psychotic, we must pretend we haven't noticed.

"But certainly for the present age," said the German biblical critic Ludwig Feuerbach (1804–72) in *The Essence of Christianity* (*Das Wesen des Christentums*, 1841), "which prefers the sign to the thing signified, the copy to the original, representation to reality, the appearance to the essence [. . .] illusion only is sacred, truth profane." Those are words from the middle of the nineteenth century. But Feuerbach's statement (translated here by George Eliot before she became a novelist) still seemed accurate to the controversial French Marxist Guy Debord (1931–94) in his much-discussed *Société du spectacle* (1967) toward the end of the twentieth. This is Debord's classic political description of modern advertising as a practice that accelerates the slippage of words from their meaning, the dominance in linguistic terms of the signifier over the signified. The vocabulary of "excellence," of "world-class," of "outstanding experience," of "the highest quality" are, for us nearly half a century after Debord, only the most obvious traces of the modern privileging of the signifier amid conceptual vacancy which we are not supposed to notice, let alone point out. Here, in advertisements, job descriptions, promotional literature, and across the internet, terms drift from their referents. We do not know if such words and phrases are describing or shaping. They form the dialect of the advertisers as well as that more recent invention, the Public Relations officer, a grand name for a propagandist (the first modern

Public Relations office was that founded by former Boston journalists as the Publicity Bureau in 1900). And one of the consequences for our relationship with time and forgetfulness of this uprooting of language is that futures, as represented in words, become even harder to know. Futures become problematic because, simply put, we can pretend we have reached where we wanted to go by merely saying that we have.

The future becomes a fictional destination when we can obtain it— the illusion or spectacle of having obtained it—by sleight of hand. If the aim of this institution or that business is to become "world class," the easiest way to attain that future it is to say, simply, that it is already. An aspiration, which might in some concrete way be testable, can be reached in the twinkling of an eye. Modify the words on the website and the job is done. We lose the necessity of evaluating what the future can bring, of judging what an ambition might be, when we can accelerate ourselves into that unknown with well-chosen but misleading language. In a complicated but also disarmingly simple way, contemporary culture makes it unnecessary to arrive at a desired future—or properly to tell whether we have arrived there or not—because we can divert ourselves with a theatrical scene: with the announcement that we are there already.

In the protean shapes of contemporary forgetting, the future has, ironically, become something to forget. We can just make it up. We can describe our intended attainment of "aims and objectives" as previously achieved, rendering futurity redundant, an irrelevance even as it is nominally the direction of our hopes. And we can be confused about futures, and what they might look like, in another way too. We can struggle to imagine futures that are, in fact, different anyway. From one perspective, this is merely to say that there is a problem with the future because there is a problem with the terms "innovation" and "new." We might as well forget the future because it is too hard to distinguish what it could be from what has been done already, to distinguish it from the present, from how things are now. We might as well forget the future because we cannot envisage what could be genuinely original.

In creativity, in the arts, this is principally an issue of pastiche, allusion, quotation, or downright plagiarism. The late British cultural theorist and blogger, Mark Fisher, in *Ghosts of My Life: Writings on Depression, Hauntology and Lost Futures* (2014), finds these difficulties suggestively applicable to popular music. What, he asks, can really sound new now? Fisher observes the confusions between "retro" and "modern," for instance, so that what is labeled as the latter can be also described as the former. Pastiche and repetition in sound, Fisher claims, is complemented by the vanishing of cover art and liner notes—forms of self-expression that in earlier times provided visual identity to albums through which newness could be supplementarily flagged. In a grand generalization, Fisher turns this perceived state of the popular music industry into a metonym for contemporary creativity more generally and, as he sees it, their "lost futures." "Despite all its rhetoric of novelty and innovation," *Ghosts of My Life* declares, "neoliberal capitalism has gradually but systematically deprived artists of the resources necessary to produce the new." Performing musicians, particularly in the classical repertoire, are among those artists unlikely to find this entirely convincing. The search for the "new" in the performance of, say Bach or Brahms, is not the first thing desired. What is wanted is convincing musical articulacy—an understanding of a work, of phrase shapes, color, and coherence—and the technical ability to realize it. Novelists and poets, and writers more generally, assume newness as a given but have other matters to privilege: their challenge (unless they are postmodern ironists) is more to do with self-expression and authenticity, a fidelity to imaginative and intellectual impulse, and to *le mot juste*.

But there is fuzziness in futurity, a loss of horizons, nevertheless, when the creative arts struggle with what newness might be like and whether repetition or return is ironic, sincere, or a sign of impoverishment. The British cultural critic Robert Hewison, thinking about contemporary arts as well, is right to add another perspective: that modern institutional and political systems of, in effect, surveillance, impede the chances of genuine newness as well: not, here, its recognition but its existence. "When an individual or an organization is expected to take the risk of creating something new," Hewison says, examining the performance criteria of modern labor in *Cultural Capital: The Rise and Fall of Creative Britain* (2014), "there has to be trust in what they are doing. The process of target-setting and audit [stifles] the independence that was needed to engender the free-ranging creativity that cultural investment was supposed to make possible." Target setting, Hewison is correct to observe, confines behaviors and limits the scope of imaginative and intellectual thought. It replaces what we think we could do—what we speculate and hope—with a potentially curtailing list of what others expect us to do.

And the problem, beyond this, of simply *identifying* the new, of recognizing it when we see it, continues. This modern contradiction is apparent not in creativity only but in the small spaces in which "newness" can be defined more generally. In commodity capitalism, the new can so often be a return to the old. This departure-as-return might consist, for instance, in the deployment of a long-dead founder's promise of quality as the new tagline for a contemporary version of the same business. Whittard, the coffee company started in Chelsea, London, in 1886, currently presents its original quality promise, made a year before Queen Victoria had been half a century on the throne, on its plastic carrier bags. Here, plainly, the new advertising strategy is the remembered. More often, commodity capitalism invests energy in nostalgia, where the "innovation" is, in fact, a direct and unblushing invocation of the old, like heritage paint, "traditional" recipes, "folk" styles of manufacturing furniture or fabrics—the distant inheritors of William Morris. These are manifestations of the same impulse that expresses itself in the modern fondness for costume drama, for *Downton Abbey* and *Foyle's War*. Here are lively topics for Gary Cross, the Penn State University professor who specializes in the history of consumption. Cross's *Consumed Nostalgia: Memory in the Age of Fast Capitalism* (2015) is a witty analysis of collectors, "nostalgia products," and Disney souvenirs in an age that cannot, Cross thinks, remember much else.

High fashion alludes to earlier designs just as scenes in films are often parodic of others; celebrity chefs return to cookery books from the 1950s or what are allegedly family or cultural traditions for ideas; property developers produce new properties, even entirely new estates, which look identical to those already existing. New airports, new finance deals, new supermarkets: they can be indistinguishable from ones we already know. The "new" idea for this institution, this traffic problem, or that school curriculum can turn out to be more or less a replica of what had been achieved in the past.

Tangible objects do something peculiar to our perception of time by inhibiting our ability to comprehend the new, even when those objects genuinely are new. The overproduction of the original can reduce our capacity to recognize it, or certainly to care very much about it. That is peculiarly true, despite John Ruskin's hopes in 1849, in relation to architecture. Rather than being, with poetry, one of the two strong conquerors of the forgetfulness of men, the modern urban and particularly metropolitan architecture now cohabits with, and helps propagate, Lethean infirmity of mind. That is partly because the mega-cities of the modern world form topographies that cannot be kept in our heads because they are too extensive to know, let alone remember. And, as with our temporary knowledges of computer systems, the modern city alters, often on a week-by-week basis. Individual buildings, landscapes, and skylines change. We can't remember cities because they are never the same.

The London skyline, to take just one example, is not in any coherent or professional sense planned. It is, as the multitude of giant cranes confirm, the site of rival projects, often huge glass and steel structures hailed as innovative skyscraper environments or high-rise residential spaces with unique characters and views (though it is true that the term "high rise," redolent of 1960s tower blocks, is now out-of-date). The vistas from the top of such creations are familiar as promised benefits to purchasers or tenants. Yet the views are changing. Among recent new constructions in the British capital are, for instance, 8 Canada Square (2002); 30 St. Mary Axe ("The Gherkin") (2003); Broadgate Tower (2008); Heron Tower (2011); The Shard (2012); St. George Wharf Tower (2013); 122 Leadenhall Street ("The Cheese Grater") (2014); 20 Fenchurch Street ("The Walkie-Talkie") (2014). But, rather like the store that is crowded with an overwhelming number of new lines, the freshness and imaginative creativity of these structures can easily cease fully to register. What we can see, as if through cataracts, is hazy because we cannot quite recall what is different this time. Continual invention becomes a strange hindrance to the recognition of invention.

Beyond commodities and Canary Wharf, beyond innovation's capacity to wear down an ability to distinguish what is innovative, there are other uncertainties about how futurity is knowable. The hiding of a return within the language of fresh starts, of new beginnings, is not confined to marketers and advertisers. Management innovation is a professional practice where we can familiarize ourselves with a further way in which the "new" is a category error. That is because there are significant impediments to defining what the scope for invention actually is. Although there might be an institutional welcome to a "new broom," a change of leadership, what can often follow is a revelation of the limited opportunities for that broom to sweep. New leaders endeavor to make their mark and, certainly, they often discover that institutional traditions, in-house patterns of thinking and historic loyalties, produce serious constraints on what they can achieve. But there is a more challenging issue in complex institutions and businesses that concerns what new leadership can initiate, and what, more generally, "newness" looks like. "Fresh" ways of management are not infrequently returns to, or revisitations of, earlier ways, even though they are not, of course, described as such. The Chief Executive Officer who determines that more resources must be spent on "frontline" activity is, for example, followed by one who decides that such activity would be enhanced by more resources in "backroom" management and administration. When he or she moves on, a third CEO might well find the only real space for innovation, for being different, is to return to the original priority. His or her language will no doubt invoke newness, presenting him or herself as leading an innovative strategic plan for a stronger future. But actually the future is, literally, the past.

Those who regret lost futures as a condition of the modern world—Mark Fisher among them, with his hope for more innovative creativity—belong, still, within the dominant patterns of future thinking. They perceive today as unable to move forward to a fresh identity, unable to be innovative, unable to make a break with the past. And breaking with the past is exactly what they want. Mourning the unobtainable new, they extend the cultural coding of yesterday as a dead weight and as history only as something to pull us down. As in psychotherapy, the critics of lost futures discern that the innermost problem with the present moment is history. In describing lost futures, those who anticipate no change are hoping that modernity will rediscover the possibilities of real innovation—and know those innovations as new when they arrive. This is no counterargument to, or rebellion against, the attachment of the present to the future.

So where *can* there be rebellion against the futures-oriented? What might such rebellion look like? "I have come to think," Marguerite Yourcenar has the Emperor say in her novel, *Memoirs of Hadrian* (1951), her grand defense of the melancholy of the ancient world: "I have come to think that great men are characterized precisely by the extreme position which they take, and that their heroism consists in holding to that extremity throughout their lives." That describes no feature of the rebels against modern forgetfulness that I can imagine. Extreme positions are not on offer in a futures-driven modernity that has so comprehensively defended itself against alternatives (except perhaps monasticism or nomadic wandering). What can a dissenter from the future, a person who hopes to find enduring value and secure identity in the best achievements of the past, obtain in the face of a contemporary culture that privileges being different but only on certain terms, and, anyway, ensures that it is hard to ascertain exactly what *is* different?

The toughest trouble for nonconformists under these circumstances is that they can easily be coded in some of the culture's most unappealing terms. To venture to declare, even modestly, that there might be value in what has been done earlier that is not merely commercial—does not simply consist of the heritage sites of tourist boards or "traditional" ranges of the supermarkets—is customarily to invite disapprobation or the assumption that one is "out-of-date." Such individuals are, supposedly, backward looking, stuck-in-the-past, retrogressive. Our synonyms for "caring about history" are generally pejorative or patronizing (like "culture vulture"). Revolt against the future-oriented is, without much effort, transformed into sentimentality or "conservatism" (when the word is negative) so that the rebel feels not only different but also belated; not alternative but irrelevant. It is one of the most striking ironies of the futures-driven contemporary world that it has largely silenced opposition by promoting difference, by apparently privileging thinking "outside-the-box," and breaking away— supposedly—from norms as principles at the heart of its values. Being different is what is good. But it is good only if difference occurs along specific lines. New ideas must not be resistant to the core principles of modernity's established ones. We are supposed to be different and new but only so long as our difference does not involve challenging the privileging of newness and of difference. We cannot be new by proposing that we stop caring so much about the new. Thinking outside of the box (*OED* dates the appearance of that phrase to 1971) is, that's to say, to be encouraged in these agreed patterns of thought—only so long as the thinking is not outside the box.

4

Forgetfulness in contemporary cultural narratives

"I don't know if you will believe me, but I do not recognize people
in the street to whom I was introduced only a month before. In
addition, I completely forget my own works. This winter I reread
one of my novels—Crime and Punishment—which I wrote ten
years ago, and more than two thirds of the novel was completely
unfamiliar to me, just as if I had not written it, to such an extent
had I managed to forget it."

FYODOR MIKHAILOVICH DOSTOYEVSKY
in a letter to Leonid Vasilyevich on March 27, 1878

There were four kinds of discrimination identified by Great Britain's
Equality Act of 2010, which covers inequity of treatment in many
forms. This is, to date, the most recent legal effort in the countries
of the British Union—it replicates the provisions of European Union
equality law— to ensure equality not only in the workplace but also
everywhere. (Note that Great Britain is, of course, different from the
United Kingdom and that the law is not identical in Northern Ireland.)
The four kinds of discrimination include "harassment." And that, like

all the act's categories of discrimination, can relate to age. Harassment on the basis of age occurs, as the act says, when "unwanted conduct related [to how old a person is] has the purpose or effect of violating [that individual's] dignity or creating an intimidating, hostile, degrading, humiliating or offensive environment." The legal formulation does not only pertain to the *old*, to be sure. It refers, explicitly, to the more general category of age, whatever it is, as a ground for discrimination (alas, the verb "to discriminate" has become almost wholly negative in contemporary English). There are occasions when the young are intimidated on the grounds of years; the middle-aged as well. "Too young for promotion" is a common act of discrimination. But in practice the majority of issues are not where the main hitch is youth or middle years. Most usually, the difficulties are for those with gray hair.

No doubt each generation has wondered whether the old folk were treated better in the past than they are now. Shakespeare, writing *King Lear* (1606), clearly thought the maltreatment of those of advanced years could be dated to well before the Christianization of the British Isles. Yet the modern West has an extreme version of this commonplace speculation. The biblical Job was correct when he said that "great men are not always wise: neither do the aged always understand judgment" (Job 32:9). But the idea that the older generations could potentially help us, that they could be wise if not every time, seems largely to have gone where the dead leaves go.

The London-based charity HelpAge International puts a consequence of that bluntly. "We believe," the organization declares on its online mission statement, "that the contribution older people make to society is invaluable. Yet older people remain some of the poorest and most neglected in the world." The depressing state of the United Kingdom's old people's homes is one small indicator of this widespread recognition. Without cultural values that invite respect, visits to such places are an effort. Beyond them, the men and women who might constitute some form of antidote, at least locally and personally, against cultural forgetting, a source of guidance and ideas, are in danger of being forgotten themselves. In dispensing with the old, modernity replicates in miniature its more extensive gestures against histories altogether, the substance of identities and minds built through acquaintance with the past. "Loneliness is a massive issue for people in later life in the UK," reported the charity Age UK in 2014: "Half of all people aged 75 and over live alone, and 1 in 10 people aged 65 or over say they are always or often feel lonely—that's just over a million people. Shockingly, half of all older people consider the television their main form of company." Elihu in the Book of Job (32:4) did not, as I said, risk being the first to speak to his elders. But now there appears to be more than 1 million people in the United Kingdom to whom pretty much nobody does.

The negative coding of the aged is self-evident, a localized but still indicative feature of modernity's intemperate view of anything past. Shakespeare gave to the world in his pastoral romance *As You Like It* (c.1599) a well-remembered formulation of human life as a sequence of Seven Stages (the theatrical pun is plain). The final stage was a return to childhood in senility. "Last scene of all," says the melancholy Jacques in Shakespeare's play, with another theatrical term,

> That ends this strange eventful history,
> Is second childishness and mere oblivion,
> Sans teeth, sans eyes, sans taste, sans everything.
>
> (Act 2, sc. 7, ll. 163–6)

This model of human life has persisted into modernity. Douwe Draaisma, the Dutch academic psychologist, is not wrong to observe in *The Nostalgia Factory: Memory, Time and Ageing* (2008) that "no matter how many vigorous, healthy and active elderly people we see around us, in developing a perspective on old age we still adhere quite closely to the image drawn or painted the sixteenth and seventeenth centuries as the 'staircase of Life' or 'Ages of Man.'" Financial forecasts concerning the sustainability of the UK's National Health Service (NHS), the nation's publicly funded health provision, are precarious, it is familiar to hear, in part because patients live longer. This is the most commonplace language coding the old primarily as a problem. The seventh stage is more protracted than others. The NHS's long-term future, in the priorities of these modern representations, is threatened by those born before it was invented. A small feature of modernity's general habit of dispensing with history is played out on the bodies—and the attendant financial burdens—of still-living parents and grandparents. The precariousness of Western nations' finances more amply is, it is equally a commonplace to assert, a result in part of the increasing number of elderly people drawing on national state pensions and/or private schemes and/or philanthropic establishments. When the Prussian statesman and Chancellor of the unified Germany, Otto von Bismarck (1815–98), introduced 65 as the retirement age in Germany, the average life expectancy for men was understood to be 66. But now the pensionable period can be nearly as long as the period worked.

Pension reform, including modifications to employee and employer contributions, and increases to retirement ages, frame the old primarily as difficulties. Almost anything from the past, including living people, are marked as spent—and we are reminded of what must be spent *on* them. After the 2008 financial crash and subsequent austerity regimes, political analysts spoke of a "lost generation." The middle-aged and the retired had, they declared, obtained a level of material success that their children and grandchildren would not approach. The older men and women of advanced economies had raided the bank and their successors would be obliged to pay for it.

The standard contemporary assumption that children could, let alone should, achieve a higher quality of life (in material terms) than that of their parents has gone. Possibly, it has gone forever. And this is the fault of the greedy old. We know of them now almost exclusively in terms of trouble.

And, sometimes, it is not only the old who are envisaged as a weight but also the living as a whole. The future is so important that even the present can be rendered irrelevant or an encumbrance except in relation to what is to come. George Osborne, MP, when serving as British Chancellor of the Exchequer, repeated a new catchphrase while delivering his controversial Budget of March 2016: "putting the next generation first." It was a rhetorical formulation that attempted to justify further cuts to national expenditure by privileging not simply the young but, presumably, the unborn as the beneficiaries of a plan. History was nowhere—and the living were transformed into agents who would bring about a supposedly better tomorrow but not for themselves.

Turned into an impediment, the "pensioners" (a familiar word that distracts us from thinking of elderly men and women except in terms of how they are funded) become distanced from those who are not. Family and friends are coerced into modernity's general distaste for history. Customary representations of the aged ensure that we comprehend them as a form of deficit, as well, perhaps literally, a cause of it. Those representations establish a valuable psychological division, even as they also separate us from those who might need help, or, it might be, could help us. The impulses of the modern world resist comprehension of forerunners as valuable, or a point from which to calibrate identity, just as they also resist identifying value in the achievements and meanings of the past more amply. Framing the elderly, particularly those in impoverished circumstances, as an obstacle in both physical and financial terms is the most obvious evidence of modernity's preference for looking to the future and its concomitant privileging of youth. But in the cultural prominence of tales of senility, of the loss of elderly minds, more suggestive matters are evident, more complexly tangled features of modernity's broader disinclination to retain the past within its vectors of thought.

Cultural as well as personal anxieties are evident in the narratives I'd now like to consider, the plural acts of medical or therapeutic issues that have become a familiar portion of today's conception of the old. But those anxieties are present obliquely rather than clearly. The narratives and cultural preoccupations with dementia and its related conditions, together with those of a small group of other medicalized topics that involve forgetting, are not empirical accounts of disease or decay alone. They are translucent not transparent: they reveal for us, if we can read what is almost invisible, elements of the modern world's relationship with time in its most extended sense. These narratives are extrusions of a cultural conscience and consciousness, a dim and fugitive awareness—smuggled into headline concerns and particular concatenations of medical bother—of what we have done to ourselves.

Modernity has not invented the diseases, and medical events, which take away our minds. Dementia, Alzheimer's, stroke, and epilepsy are not in any empirical sense pathologies of today (though it is true that extended life expectancies may make us all more prone to the first two and thus they are numerically more common). But their representative prominence, their familiarity in our contemporary world, is a Freudian slip of the tongue, a *lapsis linguae*, which reveals subconscious collective fretfulness about ample, and enduring, conceptions of memory. Emphysema and bronchitis, according to the Office of National Statistics, killed more men in 2012 in the United Kingdom than stroke or dementia/Alzheimer's (neither of these last two is fatal on its own but both inevitably lead to conditions that are).

Yet dementia and Alzheimer's are more detectable in cultural representations including media accounts of the present day's medical challenges. The Alzheimer's Society of the United Kingdom estimated in 2014 that 650,000 people in England suffer from dementia, 62 percent of them with Alzheimer's (that, by the way, is nearly as many people thought in 2016 to be autistic in the United Kingdom). In the United States, the Alzheimer's Foundation of America, the slogan of which is aptly "Memory Concerns? You're Not Alone," observed in 2016 that "it is estimated that as many as 5.1 million Americans may have Alzheimer's disease." A normal condition of a failing memory can signify the commencement of the radical loss of self through the vanishing of a personal past and with it the identity of an individual.

There cannot be many people ignorant of what this mental decline, an unanchoring of recollection, looks like, the result of a protein building in the brain that blocks the transmission of neurological information. My father traveled to visit a friend. The friend, who had long ago retired as a lawyer, was sitting in his own home in his own armchair. Everything was familiar, warm, and normal. The conversation was familiar, warm, and normal. But then it flagged. "I like the picture of the mountain," my father said, encouragingly. He was looking at one of the reproductions of paintings on the sitting room wall. "It's odd," said my father's companion, gazing around him with wonder. "I've the same pictures in my own house." It was a terrible moment when my father realized that a friend had ceased to be.

Dementia and its anguishes have expanded from medicine to art just as they occupy a conspicuous place in print and digital media. The literary critic John Bayley, to whom I have already referred, succeeded in making readers remember his wife, the Irish philosopher and novelist Iris Murdoch (1919–99), more for her dementia than her fiction. It was an odd kind of marital revenge. But Bayley's publishers clearly understood the viable nature of this medical form of forgetfulness in the literary marketplace. Celebrity dementia makes for sellable narratives. And occasionally a diagnosis provokes some national anxiety. It was left to the *New York Times* on March 30, 2015, to reassure a general readership that language analysts had confirmed that Ronald Reagan (1911–2004) did not have traces of dementia sufficient to impede his judgment while serving as the fortieth president of the United States. Reagan at the White House was still more or less himself, secure in his own personal history and personality. But now the histories of more ordinary lives have caught up with those of the famous.

Christine Zimmerman's *Beyond Forgetting* (2014) is the story of a regular young American woman who was obliged to abandon her college studies to care for her grandfather with Alzheimer's. The book, says CreateSpace Independent Publishing Platform, which issued it, provides "a rare insight into an often-closed moment in the hardest part of many people's lives." Sadly, the insights are no longer rare because they are, indeed, the story of "many people's lives." Chris Carling's *But Then Something Happened: A Story of Everyday Dementia* (2012), Marianne Sciucco's *Blue Hydrangeas: An Alzheimer's Love Story* (2013), Vanessa Luther's *A Life Stolen: My Father's Journey through Alzheimer's* (2014), or Jill Stoking's *Joan's Descent into Alzheimer's* (2014) are among other volumes that relate "ordinary" failures of mind. They are compounds of memoir and fiction, commemorating the identity of those who can remember themselves no longer. The book shelves are stacked with what is passing away.

The cinema relates narratives of Alzheimer's too. *Age Old Friends* (1989), for instance, or *Firefly Dreams* (2001), *Iris: A Memoir* (2001) after Bayley's books, *A Song for Martin* (2001), *The Notebook* (2004), *Aurora Borealis* (2006), *Away from Her* (2007), *The Savages* (2007). The screen has transformed forgetfulness into spectacle. In both written and visual narrative, madness has been lifted from the Athenian stage and turned into the mundane, poignant, and simply sad. But the modern attraction to these histories of loss, to the erasure of memories and selves, is not simply because they are common. It is because, in a veiled but still legible manner, such narratives are cautiously, covertly, self-reflective. In the histories of men and women breaking their connections with the past, with memory and themselves, is a pathologized version, I think, of modern culture and what it has done, or tries to do, to those who live under its glaucomic gaze. These are stories of what happens to identities without memory: human episodes of culture's more general objection to looking behind. Alzheimer's is not only a disease that is common, as well as peculiarly frightening. Its representational presence hints, coyly, at a truth about how today feels for individuals living forgetfully among the values we have constructed. We may be terrified of dementia because it is widespread and its affects are catastrophic. But the fear arises also because we are half-conscious, as dutiful forward-facing citizens of modernity, that we figuratively have it already.

The Scottish journalist and broadcaster Sally Magnusson, writing *Where Memories Go: Why Dementia Changes Everything* (2013), remarks that watching her mother's illness obliged her to reflect on what it meant to be human. Where is the point in dementia's decline, Magnusson inquires, when a man or a woman stops being a man or a woman? At what point, in other words, does the departure of history deliver a fatal blow to identity? It is an uncomfortable question both for an individual and a culture. The same can be said of the sudden infliction of a severe stroke: who is it that is left? Ischemic and hemorrhagic strokes, the two versions of this siderant event now understood by medical science, damage the functioning of the brain because, like Alzheimer's, they kill off its living tissue. Every year, says the (British) Stroke Association, there are "approximately 152,000 strokes in the UK; that's one every 3 minutes 27 seconds." The American Stroke

Association tells of a more frequent occurrence. "About 795,000 Americans each year suffer a new or recurrent stroke," the association reported in 2016: "This means, on average, a stroke occurs every 40 seconds." Stroke is the number four killer in the United States. And in turn, few citizens of either nation state can be unaware of its threat, its causes, and its damage. Stroke narratives, the representations of its sufferers, are as familiar as aspirin.

Stroke does not always kill. And histories of recovery have both their own reassurance and marketability too. As it happens, I am writing this book after surviving a stroke, which occurred on October 16, 1998, in my kitchen in Oxford. I know for certain why a stroke has such a name because the event feels like exactly that: a blow to the head, a blow *inside* the head. Physiologically I have more or less recovered except, pointedly enough, for a weakened memory and, strange to say, slightly altered handwriting. I am not quite the person as I used to sign myself. Psychologically, however, I have not stopped thinking about that early autumn morning when my world, as well as my kitchen, spun: the threat of losing myself, departing from my past, has been too troubling to erase.

High-profile individuals have written and spoken fully about the healing that can occur even after a severe ischemic or hemorrhagic attack. Andrew Marr, for example, the Scottish journalist who was blighted by a stroke in January 2013, was discussing what had happened to him in TV interviews and in press articles by the end of the same year. He has now returned at work, to all appearances, well. Earlier, Robert McCrum, the English writer and journalist, who had endured a devastating stroke in 1995, remembered the long progress of recuperation in his wryly titled *My Year Off: Recovering Life after a Stroke*, published in 1998. Sharon Stone, the American actress, spoke candidly to the British popular newspaper *The Daily Express* in February 2015 about the protracted two-year process of recovering from her severe stroke in 2001. Stone had had to learn to walk again. Nearly 15 years later, she was still being asked about it.

Such sufferers are human beings remembering pain. But their narratives, and the cultural prominence of them, are also small but noticeable signs of modernity's relationship with memory more generally and its encoded, fitful aspirations for recovery. With the case of strokes, the most valuable necessity for restoration is time. The human brain, over weeks and months, sometimes over years, heals what it can. Sometimes physiotherapy is needed, sometimes speech therapy. But the key is patience. What can be mended will be: by the body, largely by itself. But waiting—the virtues of passivity, patience, and stamina—will not assist the broader restoration of a culture that is building a wall between itself and yesterday. Stroke-recovery narratives do stealthy work. They tell us literally that strokes need not kill. But they also cipher unfocused longings, cultural ambitions against the grain, that we might, somehow, rise above our modern predicament, our externally driven condemnation to forgetfulness, and reconnect with pasts again. We might find how the achievements of history profit or enrich us (it is unfortunate that both those terms are now verbs primarily concerning the increase of material wealth). Stroke narratives, circulating through print, cinemas, and electronic media, process an understanding beneath modernity's love affair with futurity, that continuation with histories is necessary to stable identities, both personal and cultural—to fullness, security, and wholeness. Stroke becomes, however mistily, a figure of what modernity is doing to us and how we would like, not only for ourselves but also collectively, to convalesce.

Stroke-recovery narratives, like the histories of recuperation told in the neurologist Oliver Sacks's book *Awakenings* (1973), intrigue in part because they are episodes of coming back to oneself. Here are implicitly representations of men and women rejoining history and in turn are microcosms of more substantial cultural aspirations for root-edness. For the survivors of the *encephalitis lethargica* epidemic of the 1920s, Sacks was able to induce a recovery, albeit nearly half a century after the infection and one that was partial, temporary, sometimes terrible, and always too late. Recovery of a sort it was, nevertheless. "Mrs. B." was among Sacks's patients. She became for him, as the medical profession likes to phrase it, a "case study." "Mrs. B." was given the seemingly miraculous psychoactive drug L-DOPA and, shortly afterward, she was able "to hold a pencil in her right hand," Sacks writes, "and to make a first entry in her diary." This entry, we read, was "her name, followed by the comment, 'It is twenty years since I have written. I'm afraid I have almost forgotten how to write my name.'" Mrs. B.'s name comes back and so, for a short while, does Mrs. B.: through a new wonder chemical, she temporarily finds herself again because she can remember who she was. Such histories plot a (qualified) marvel of medicine. But they also adumbrate the half-recognized desires of forgetful inhabitants of the contemporary world to reconnect with history, to reacquire the testimony of ages once more.

Nowhere is the modern realization of the loss of history more complicatedly transformed, more complexly scattered in cultural representations, than in today's shared fascination with cognitive disorders. The conversion of autism (the name comes from the ancient Greek for the "self," αὐτο, *auto*) into a spectrum disorder significantly increased the number of individuals diagnosed with it. Empirically, there were about 700,000 diagnosed autistic individuals in the United Kingdom in 2015—but that is only the number of those with an official label. The condition was first named in 1943 by the Austrian-American psychiatrist Leo Kanner (1894–1981) (pronounced "Carner"). But he conceived it as a single state: a patient either was autistic or not. Autism's recategorization as a spectrum meant that diagnosis became more of a judgment, a weighing of sometimes conflicting evidence.

Rather than a condition that was self-declaring, autism required a diagnostic process that was something of an art (and it should be added that we may only have the first clue as to whether there is a range of cognitive disorders that are peculiar to girls and for which current paradigms, largely predicated on male subjects, do not work). Whatever the case, as Richard Panek and Temple Grandin observe in *The Autistic Brain: Exploring the Strength of a Different Kind of Mind* (2013), the disorder in all its plurality involves mental habits that exist in an exceptionally wide diversity of individuals. "At one end of the spectrum," Panek and Grandin say, "you might find the severely disabled. At the other end, you might encounter an Einstein or a Steve Jobs." The same essential indicators relate to near-complete dysfunctionality as well as to *savant* or genius.

The common and now, so to speak, colloquialized nature of this disorder—"on the spectrum" has become a familiar conversational comment in many discussions of what other people are like—has driven the proliferation of both medical interest and, in its wake, cultural representations. And these have, in turn, helped further propel medical investigation. But the diverse narratives and representative practices are, as with dementia and stroke, penetrated by meanings that are a portion of that same cultural conscience, a segment of modernity's awareness of its self and its fractious, amnesiac relation to history at levels beyond the individual mind. One psychological theory (as distinct from physiological or psychiatric) that endeavors to account for the un- or antisocial dimension of autism—its self-contained nature and, as it were, "me-ness"—proposes that autistic individuals lack a "Theory of Mind" (ToM). For the British Romantic poet Samuel Taylor Coleridge (1772–1834), this would have been called the "Sympathetic Imagination." It is the ability to conceive how the world might look to someone else. Coleridge rightly regarded the Sympathetic Imagination as a necessary moral as well as a social faculty. Men and women, he declared, fall rapidly into conflict and alienation if they do not consider perspectives other than their own. That, to a point, is the "moral" of Coleridge's celebrated ballad, "The Rime of the Ancient Mariner" (1798/1834). Yet for autistic individuals, without a ToM, awareness of others' perspectives is, it seems, cognitively unachievable.

As the British autism expert Simon Baron-Cohen explains, this problem can be especially evident in those with Asperger's syndrome. In fact, this condition is one that the American Psychiatric Association no longer recognizes. The association removed it from its influential (and controversial) *Diagnostic and Statistical Manual of Mental Disorders* (DSM-5) in 2013. But Asperger's remains a helpful category in European diagnoses and in general conversation on both sides of the Atlantic. This high-functioning disorder—it is named after the Austrian doctor Hans Asperger (1906–80) who first described it—is strongly associated with an advanced level of system-making. And other people get in the way of systems. Lacking a ToM, the individual with Asperger's has knowledge of potentially terrifying difference, of individuals who are threatening because they do things differently. Other people literally change physically ordered things, like color-coded book spines, or they have different opinions about the world generally.

Medical and educational authorities, Baron-Cohen remarks, "need to keep in mind that many people with Asperger syndrome dream of a planet where they are the only human being, where there are no interruptions, where events happen with regularity and predictability. Many pine for the lifestyles that were adopted by monks in monasteries, where a calm tranquility allowed for routines in domestic life combined with solitary work." It is a yearning for a way of life from the Age of Faith where a ToM would be unnecessary. Actually, this is misleading. The monasteries were attentive to the past and maintained their traditions and collective ways of being. But the long-ing of those with Asperger's syndrome, as Baron-Cohen narrates it, is not to be collective or to undertake anything shared at all. It is simply to be left alone.

Extreme conditions of autism lead to narratives of exceptional social disjunction, involving individuals with a cognitive inabil-ity to recognize the existence of others except in relation directly to what those others offer. (One of the largest killers of autistic individuals, after epilepsy and heart disease, is suicide—a form of death that is peculiarly unaware of others.) These narratives pre-sent us with individuals seemingly living with a terror of innova-tion, a grave inability to accommodate change. "Most researchers," Richard Panek and Temple Grandin assert, "can't imagine living a life in which every novel situation, threatening or not, is fueled by an adrenaline rush." Following an unchanging routine, in ways determined long before, is the only security. Autistic individu-als, in turn, are quietly emblematic counters to the entrepreneur. They embody, unknowingly, a refusal of modernity's preference for transformation, for thinking "outside the box," and strangely con-test contemporary capitalism's habit of believing in new departures. Amid the obligatory celebration of innovators, the severely autistic person is the most visible way of being antithetical to invention within medicalized representations. His or her story is a narrative embodiment of what would be nothing less than modern capi-talism's nemesis: a failure to move on, an inability to "grow" or "develop." But what is important, culturally, is that in such autism histories the refusal to innovate is, of course, a marker of an incur-able disorder. Being resistant to change, in these clinical histories, is diagnostic evidence of something irretrievably wrong. Modernity's values are smuggled in, and reprised, in this narrative admonish-ment of what would supposedly undo us all.

Simultaneously, however, the autistic individual hyperbolizes rather than resists an essence, as well as a fear, of the modern. Autism narratives present us with the extremity of a consciousness that has almost no relationship with the past, and where identity, as a result, emerges as far less complex or complete. It is easy for anyone to be oppressed by an expectation that his or her life should make sense, be in a deep way coherent. But the autistic individual's wholeness—if that is what it is—seems to be distractingly simple. That wholeness, it may be, is not an oppressive expectation but a given: a set of desires and fears, without much, or any, possibility of change. Modernity advises its citizens that history of all kinds must be discarded unless it can be privatized, personalized, or sold. The autism narrative, about those who do not change, cannot change, or are terrified of change, sketches out a Gothic inversion of the contemporary West's relationship with time.

For those at the severest end of the spectrum, history does not appear to register at all except in a severely incomplete sense. It is hard to know with extreme cases of autism whether memory does more than retain knowledge of the routines and rhythms of daily life that must be followed for security. It is hard to know whether experience registers as anything other than that divided between the reassuringly consistent and the appallingly new. Care for the history of others' lives, whatever the case, is apparently completely absent. In turn, the autistic individual fascinates, and is narrativized in fiction and film, in part because he or she surreptitiously encodes a collective realization—a feature of the communal conscience—that to live apart from history is not to be fully human. That realization is disguised a little, kept at arm's length, by the current cultural preference for representations, particularly on screen, of autism as a source of unusual gifts and exceptional powers. We are half-distracted from what autism might figure of ourselves by spectacles of weird brilliance. "It would be nice," remarked *The Guardian* newspaper on March 9, 2016, weary of this phenomenon where children were concerned, "to see an autistic kid in a drama who is not a prodigy." We can shield ourselves from too much realization of our own cognitive obstacles, our own limited comprehension of pasts, by dwelling primarily on quirky genius.

Dementia has as yet no cure—though apparently significant drug experiments take place. No pill, cream, or injection exists, either, which can alter an autistic person into a neurotypical, normal individual. Modernity itself may well have no cure, and its capacity to negate and even pathologize objection is daunting. We can sense the outline of a cultural conscience, nevertheless, in the unspoken terms, the half-hidden implications, of those prominent medical narratives. We can discern, if we can read the parapraxis of modernity's clinical fascinations, that there is a comprehension of what is happening. And it maybe we can perceive the penetration of modernity's primary values in prominent therapeutic practices too. Even the cures for some of our modern states of mind mirror and indirectly reenact, like the play-within-a-play in *Hamlet,* the central drama of our difficulties.

Psychoanalysis, Cognitive Behavioral Therapy (CBT), and Gestalt counseling belong, in particular, with modernity's priorities plainly enough because their object of study is the individual and his or her inner life. Those practices, that is to say, are the therapeutic by-products of capitalism, the nineteenth-century world of advertising, and the twentieth-century world of public relations, simply in their attentiveness to the desires of private persons and the satisfaction of those desires. Where the agents of commodity capitalism aspire to persuade us that we have a right to own those shoes or that new model of cell phone, these therapeutic practices operate on the cognate principle that we are each entitled to be happy and to be listened to. Their assumption is that we have a right to have our emotional needs met, and our point of view heard and taken into account.

Gestalt counseling in particular offers affirmation that a "client"—
the term exposes the financially transactional relationship—has an
advocate in the counselor, the person who will assure them that it
is understandable to feel as they do and right to express it. Gestalt
counseling, perhaps, stands in for what we might hope from a perfect
friend: the idealized person, a fiction of commodity capitalism, who
is entirely on our side and supportive of our needs as well as free from
their own.

But, beyond this, therapeutic practice in psychology, broadly
defined, inherits and reconfigures modernity's priorities in other ways.
Psychoanalysis, CBT, and Gestalt counseling are marked by the traces
of a suspicion of history and at times by its pathologization. The development of CBT is what Dana Becker, Professor of Social Work at Bryn
Mawr, accurately regards in *One Nation under Stress: The Trouble with
Stress as an Idea* (2013), as part of the expansion of the psychological
professions in the 1980s and their promotion of, in Becker's simple but
crucial words, a "therapeutic culture that embraces an interventionist
perspective." CBT, that is to say, belongs among contemporary procedures of mental health care predicated on a (capitalist) assumption that there is something wrong with an individual if he or she is
unhappy, rather than with the culture in which that person lives or,
bluntly phrased, the nature of being human. Important within the
assumptions of CBT, in addition, is that which is coherent with the
world from which it emerged: a program of breaking from the past.

CBT proposes that human beings have scripts from which, in
a manner of speaking, they read and with which they negotiate
life. These scripts contain an individual's standard or, supposedly,
"natural" response to particular kinds of events. The scripts might,
for instance, include: "If something goes wrong it is my fault;" "If
someone does not speak to me at work it means that they dislike
me;" "If someone says that they like me, they will always let me

down, so I must not let anyone become close to me." The challenge of the CBT counselor is to rewrite the script and, as a result, to release an individual from preformulated reactions to situations that distress or, more exactly, situations that preformulated reactions turn *into* distress. To achieve this rewriting or rewiring, first of all, the counselor has to reveal to clients that they *have* a script, a set pattern in their ways of thinking. And then he or she has to persuade the client that the script is not immutable. CBT endeavors to provide clients with different lines: to reorientate mental responses away from historic patterns toward new and, obviously, better ones. Instead of thinking, for instance, "If someone does not speak to me at work it means that they dislike me," there might be: "If someone does not speak to me at work, I'll speak to them first and show I am interested in them." CBT replaces, or aspires to replace, the unhelpful reactions that have governed the past with more enabling lines for the future.

It is far from an ignoble undertaking. CBT is beneficial for many and life changing for a few. Yet it is still a practice that confirms an outline of the *Ur*-narrative of modernity while transforming it into— at its best—a cure. The leading assumption of CBT is that the past is burdensome, a storm drogue on the present and the future. Its conviction is that success lies in breaking from history and that identity is not grounded in the past but made better, made happier, by rejection. CBT—a therapeutic version of Protestant iconoclasm—works with the promise of contentment, and greater respect for the self, which is derived from moving away from how things were before. Identity is not dependent on the past; indeed, preferable identities are, as St Augustine thought, discovered by discarding it. If this makes some sense in the management of particular forms of mental health and mental (as well as sometimes physical) behavior, it is also confirmation of the guiding assumption of the contemporary world in which desires and fears are formed and identities dislodged from histories.

CBT works with just-under-the-consciousness or what has become naturalized as "instinctive" thought structures. It assumes there are patterns with which we have become so familiar that we do not realize they are patterns. Freudian psychoanalysis, however, proposes more complex states of psychic existence: a less tidy paradigm of the mind, which depends on the interrelationship of the conscious, pre- or subconscious, and unconscious. Following Freud's conceptualization of the psyche, the Freudian analyst is interested in the communications between these layers of the mind—the way, for instance, that the subconscious emerges in dreams or slips of the tongue. There is not a script to be followed in this model of human psychology. But there is a relationship with history to be considered nevertheless. The American Psychoanalytic Association (APA), speaking in relation to the important psychoanalytical category of "Transference," the "projection onto another person (e.g., the analyst) of feelings, past associations, or experiences," phrases this attitude to the past in conveniently straightforward, if inelegant, terms. "Transference," the APA says, "is an important concept in psychoanalysis because it demonstrates that past experiences impact the present. Interpreting transference in the psychoanalytic setting can shed light on unresolved conflicts."

Freudian models of human psychology involve the assumption that progress, what Charles Darwin (1809–82) might have called more neutrally successful adaptation, resides in managing the aftershocks of past events well. Progress is a consequence of fixing what the APA labels as "unresolved conflicts," of moving beyond that peculiarly important psychoanalytical category of trauma. This word, from the Greek τραῦμα, *trauma*, a wound, first appears in an article by William James (1842–1910), the American psychologist who was the brother of the novelist Henry and diarist Alice, in 1894. Trauma, explicitly, is the damaging of the psyche by history: "A psychic injury," as *OED* puts it, "*esp.* one caused by emotional shock the memory of which is repressed and remains unhealed." Freudian and subsequent psychoanalytical paradigms in Freud's wake, propose that neuroses and psychoses—that is, disabling anxiety and loss of contact with reality—are primarily the result of not being able to move beyond, or adapt to, what is (half-) unknowingly remembered. Memory, on the couch, is always potentially impeding.

Freud's narratives of development involve scenes of potentially "primal" trauma: separation from the womb; erotic entanglement with the mother; sexual jealousy of the father. These, assembled around the explanatory myth of the Oedipus complex, can be controlled or can be the source of lifelong psychological damage. The therapist's task, working with his or her illustrative mythic paradigms, is—in its simplest terms—to identify the historic trauma and, through sustained analysis, sometimes over years or even a life time, assist the patient to reach a better accommodation with what had once happened. Here is an individual reorganizing their perspective on personal histories—or at least being encouraged to do so, for the end-point of psychoanalysis is a matter of sustained and unresolved debate. In an important sense, Freudian therapy works against the tide of modern conceptions of optimal relationships with the past because the "talking cure," as psychoanalysis is sometimes colloquially called, aspires to assimilate the patient to history, to create a more "comfortable" relationship with what previously occurred. Being "at peace" with a past event—bereavement, marriage breakdown, sexual abuse, emotional neglect—is a success narrative in psychoanalysis even if it is one that is often about-to-be rather than actually achieved. Such a process is not, regarded in this light, about denying history but, rather, keeping it in mind without being oppressed by it.

Yet psychoanalysis shares in the dominant mode of modernity's relationship with time nevertheless because it encourages concentration on histories from which the patient needs to be moved. Its fundamental ambition is to understand escape, both *from* and *to*. The traumatization, the catastrophizing, of personal history—its conversion into, or affirmation as, trouble—is a staple of the psychoanalyst's consulting room. Therapeutic practice is, in turn, imbricated with the collective principles of contemporary capitalism that perceives in the past a weight on progress, a failure to seize opportunity and, as Samuel Smiles would say, "get on." Sigmund Freud opened his consulting rooms in Vienna in 1886 in the full flood of capitalist modernity. His psychotherapeutic principles did not, of course, bring psychological trauma into existence. But his historical and cultural location, his awareness of the modern classification of history as a problem, enabled Freud peculiarly to conceptualize why "what happened before" might be a source of damage.

Something similar, on a smaller though still culturally prominent scale, is true more recently of Post Traumatic Stress Disorder (PTSD). That is a condition of mind, another form of psychic wound, first associated with veterans from the United States of America returning home from the Vietnam War (1955–75). It is no "invention" of technological modernity either. But modernity's habits of mind, the persistent forms of thought about the nature of history as disastrous, the thing to which one returns only in sickness and not in health, helped make PTSD recognizable, and label-able, in modernity's war-torn midst. More substantially, the contemporary concentration on classifying abuse—sexual, physical, emotional—has absorbed similar principles about how to read the past. Real problems are identified, of course: real abusers and real pain. But, at the conceptual level, the concentration constitutes a habit of mind fueled by the same idea that history is primarily to be regarded as that moment when things went wrong.

Medicine and therapy inform, yet are also informed by, the forces that contour our mental life. They are not detached, and what generates headlines in medicine and mental health care, as well as what is converted into fiction, film, and memoir, refract priorities different from merely abstract interest, commonness of condition, or urgency of the need for healing. Our ways of thinking about, our ways of seeing, the world are infiltrated. And some of our cultural narratives, even some of our acts of restoration, are modernity's principles reconceived. In different ways, such representations and practices both reaffirm modernity's priorities and provide us, potentially, with an opportunity to perceive them expressed. They are both replications and, at least theoretically, revelations.

The cultural conscience is hazily visible. But what—to return to my earlier question—might an overt rebellion against modernity's privileging of forgetfulness look like? Modernity's values, and their consequences, seep into lives, occupying minds, sometimes without us realizing that they are there. Could we think differently? Could we remember without needing either to catastrophize the past or sell it? Could we celebrate and explore history's best achievements, both things and acts, in ways not sentimental, profit driven, or amateur? If we cannot alter a whole culture's direction, are there ways of being more modestly different, of standing in another relationship to time and memory?

5

Learning pasts

"Repetition, if it is possible, thus makes a person happy, while recollection makes him unhappy, assuming, of course, that he actually gives himself time to live and does not, immediately upon the hour of his birth hit upon an excuse, such as that he has forgotten something, to sneak back out of life again."

SØREN KIERKEGAARD, *Repetition* (1843)

It would be easy to think that the downgrading of anything from the past that cannot be turned into money has been compounded by popular culture's general, though not exclusive, preference for the trivial, superficial, and easy. A person making that assumption might perceive in popular culture's habits of reducing the seriousness of inheritances, historical achievements, and accomplishments, a potent way in which the modern world deprives itself of the best attainments of yesterday. That person might recognize in, for example, a film version of a classic novel metonymic evidence of "dumbing down"—a term that first comes into existence in 1927 in relation, appropriately enough, to Hollywood. The British author and medical doctor Anthony Daniels, who writes cultural criticism usually under the name of Theodore Dalrymple, puts a version of this assumption in his bracing book, *Our Culture, What's Left of It: The Mandarins and the Masses* (2005). It remains, Dalrymple says, a matter of sorrow to me that, with the opportunity for individual participation in the glories of our culture greater than ever before in all our history, the meretricious, the vulgar, and the downright hideous should triumph so easily, should find so eager a reception in the minds of men.

But the trouble is not only with the impoverished portions of popular culture. Part of the barrier between ourselves and a better understanding of historical achievement, the glories of cultures, as Dalrymple phrases it, are not the people in the internet chat rooms but in the library. They are not readers of magazines but the teachers of the past. Part of the problem, it is unpleasurable to admit, is with the intellectuals.

The issue for this chapter, then, is not the pop lyric or the cartoon but the views of university-educated men and women, those possessed of a sequence of ideas that have come to signify membership of high-status groups and cultural elites (there are all kinds of problems with the term "elites" but it will have to do here). These, I think, have contributed—for reasons easy to comprehend and hard to understand—to the further vanishing of the past. It is not, in fact, only the modern-day barbarians who weaken our ability to think robustly about the achievements of historical culture: it is those who, on first glance, might have been expected to defend those achievements.

How has this happened and why? Is it peculiar to England or no? Why have the custodians of precious things—sold them?

It is necessary to turn to two distinctive moments in the recent history of ideas and in the history of liberal education, which meet in a kind of sorrowful handshake, to find the intellectual sources of this problem. Part of the conceptual basis for the reduction in the significance of history and its archives has to do with a "turn," a new direction, in the second half of the twentieth century, in the history of reading. "Reading" here is not meant to be confined to words but refers to acts of interpretation generally. The verb refers to explanations of multiple artifacts and activities: buildings as well as documents, and among other things, paintings, speeches, family traditions, the practices of daily life. This "turn" is best understood in relation to words, however, because what was proposed by a group of influential thinkers in the middle of the twentieth century concerned first of all verbal meaning: a radical break between what linguists call the "signifier" and the "signified." More simply, the assertion was that there no real or dependable relationship between a word and what it apparently meant (the advertisers had got there long before the academics). The "linguistic turn" of the second half of the twentieth century drew, for sure, on eighteenth-century ideas (and in fact on classical and medieval philosophies) about the relationship between language and reality, and on established questions about whether it was possible to describe that reality in an authoritative way. But the modern linguistic version of these ideas, concerned with the gap between a word and the *verité* it appeared to depict, produced new results. That was because the philosophy of unstable meanings obtained unusual success in influencing university departments dedicated broadly to the study of culture.

Language became perceived, for a cluster of academics and their followers, as a medium not for the expression of intention but the recognition of intention's irrelevance and, anyway, undiscoverability. "Every verbal signification lies at the confluence of countless semantic rivers," said the French philosopher Emmanuel Levinas (1906–95), describing the phenomenon that is often labeled as "poststructuralism" (though it is true, consistent with a suspicion of rooted meaning, that the poststructuralists themselves generally disliked being regarded as a unified school of thought with ideas that could be defined). Each occasion for speaking or writing was always conceived, nevertheless, as a flood of possible meanings. No single sense could be privileged, no authority, the poststructuralists of the 1980s believed, could be given to intention insofar as intention could be discerned.

The aspiration of poststructuralist readers, and those closely or loosely associated with them, was to demonstrate, essentially, the same point: that what had the appearance of meaning, what looked like a stable statement or a clear argumentative position, always betrayed itself somewhere in the midst of its articulation and collapsed. In the assumptions of what became known as "Deconstruction," forcefully developed by another French philosopher and linguist, Jacques Derrida (1930–2004), all forms of texts, each attempt by an individual human being to articulate meaning through language, was a different kind—but also the same kind—of miscarriage.

The critic's business, the intellectual's task, was to demonstrate how the slip occurred—at what point and in what way—and thus to affirm the insight of poststructuralism that meaning suffused words to such an extent that no utterance could pin it down. Deconstruction's arguments are plural, diverse, complex—yet they are also disarmingly simple. The interpretative loop—the practitioners of Deconstruction generally preferred the term "hermeneutical" to "interpretative"— was closed when, as was plainly necessary, poststructuralists began to explore the failure of poststructuralism itself to make sense. It was not, after all, possible for a follower of this school to maintain that language could not articulate meaning in order to prove the correctness of a philosophy, expressed in language, which declared it. The fault lines of Deconstructionist propositions became subjects for the Deconstructionists in a peculiar kind of self-referential probing of why meaning was not possible in the documents that argued meaning was not possible.

The conviction that sense was on-the-run or always-already swamped by alternatives, that no words could signify clearly and distinctly, might seem to be such an oddity that it could not have entered the minds of serious thinkers. Such people, a visitor from another planet might reasonably have assumed, could never have been seduced by these propositions. They could not have fallen for an epistemology that declared, in language, that human beings were trapped within words which—despite poststructuralism's disavowals of authority—could authoritatively be said never to signify. But that was not the case. The assumptions of those championing the linguistic turn proved tenacious for a while in English departments, cultural studies departments, and even in parts of history departments— which might be thought to retain faith in the empirical—provoking work that ruminated on the impossibility of knowing the past, of understanding any document, except as an infinity of possible interpretations, each folding in on itself as the signifier lost contact with the signified.

A single text demonstrates, particularly in literary studies, the implications of this distinctive moment in the history of Western thought. It is a text occasionally still taught and discussed today and it still retains, albeit for a small number of people, a kind of ritualistic or totemic significance. Roland Barthes's essay "La mort de l'auteur" (1967, "The Death of the Author") was a touchstone of the intellectual decision to embrace the poststructuralist case. For a while in the 1980s, this was an almost compulsory document for anyone reading for a degree in the arts and humanities.

Barthes proposed—or rather, to be fair, he has been taken to propose, for there is an argument, ironically, over whether he quite meant what he was taken to mean—that the "Author's empire" was too powerful. Following an idea from the French Symbolist poet Stéphane Mallarmé (1842–98), "The Death of the Author" proclaimed that such rule, such authorial tyranny over a text's meaning, needed to be toppled. Too long, Barthes asserted, have readers believed that the author of what they were reading controlled the sense. We must rather, he said, substitute "language itself for the man who hitherto was supposed to own it." Language, Barthes proclaimed in that peculiarly fervent and subversive moment in modern French intellectual history, when students were literally at the barricades, "alone acts, 'performs,' and not 'oneself'." Language, for this left-wing radical who for many years struggled to find a post as an academic, could never be employed to express a mind or to understand one. The Barthesian reader, born from the apparent demise of the author, sensed only such meaning as was possible within language's endless breaking down of itself, its coincidence of multiple possibilities, its currents of signification.

For the most intellectually unresourceful readers, Barthes's essay was—and sometimes still is—taken to assert that a text means what you want it to mean. (It is curious, by the way, in the reception of this piece, how rigorously Barthes's apparent intentions have been respected—almost as an article of faith—in a document advising its reader that authorial language cannot, or should not, communicate stable, certain, or unitary meaning.) Within the canon of poststructuralist writing, Barthes became—as one of the consequences of "The Death of the Author"—a figurehead for the idea that it was impossible to value the meaning of the past. That was because, within the documents and archives of history, there was merely confirmation of meaning's incorrigible plurality. Adam Phillips observes in *One Way and Another* (2013) that it is "impossible to know the consequence of one's words," that "[learning] to listen can only be learning—if that is the right word—to bear what listening calls up in you." That, certainly, is correct. We cannot be sure that our meaning will get through or that we can deal with someone else's. But that is not to propose that there is no meaning and intention in the first place, however it might on occasions founder or be rejected. Yet what mattered, within the popular versions of poststructuralist thought, was not intention inscribed in an artifact—a document from history, say—but the reader's ability in the here and now to make that document "mean" what they wanted, thought, or whimsically desired, there and then. The past was, in this specific intellectual sense, abolished because it was never knowable.

Poststructuralism did not survive as a norm for long. It is almost unheard-of now to meet anyone who describes themselves uncritically or without qualification as a Deconstructionist—however interested and thoughtful about the Deconstructionists they might be. But something of the enduring nature of poststructuralist ideas, and their implications for how to read the past, has survived. Poststructuralism's orthodoxies are dimly felt, for instance, in the widespread popular and sometimes even academic conviction that interpreting the past is primarily to be regarded, in terms of the substance of knowledge, as a wholly subjective matter. Poststructuralism lingers in part because it gave some conceptual underpinning to the notion that, in any study of historical texts, accuracy, and veracity are unobtainable. Interpreting the past, in the least analytical versions of this understanding, is seen only as a matter of fancy. History's achievements became, at the most extreme, but the blank page on which the individual could write what they liked. In turn, historical study became problematically assumed—both by a few of its practitioners and by many of those outside—to be something that could not be taken seriously because it involved only opinion and the unstable eddying of meanings that could never be safe. Poststructuralists professionalized the language of the arts and humanities: they gave to them a *lingua franca* that required special training to comprehend. But, however paradoxical it sounds, the poststructuralists also guaranteed that those disciplines would become regarded as amateur intellectual pursuits, as matters without rigor or meaningful contribution to the nature, achievements, and identity of cultures.

The after-effects of the linguistic turn have contributed to the reduction, in the academic perception, of the seriousness of historical study in its broadest sense. This reduction is an intellectual version, perhaps, of the widespread popular acceptance that an interest in the achievements of the past is only to be comprehended when it is labeled as, for instance, a "hobby," an "enthusiasm," or a "past time." When John Beale decided punningly to call his retro or vintage gift shop in the United Kingdom—selling imitation Celtic broaches, look-a-like Victorian nightshirts, and CDs of songs from the 1950s—"Past Times," he did not know it but he was reflecting what was happening in arts and humanities departments.

But if poststructuralism damaged a public conception that the past can be a topic of serious knowledge and study, the dominance of liberal ideas about history has, in addition, persuaded subsequent intellectuals and many of those taught by them, that the safest and most self-affirming posture to adopt toward the past is one of criticism. This is an idea that has intersected with the problems caused by the linguistic turn. Liberal attitudes to the study of historical achievement have now sufficiently installed themselves into intellectual life, and in the political, critical, and cultural assumptions of those educated within the (neo-)liberal tradition, that they have become almost impossible to question. These attitudes have obtained the curious condition of being a status marker, an indicator in themselves of a particular educational background. A moral certainty has attended some of the assumptions, too, which has problematized debate further because the weakest of liberal minds has been able to defend itself against criticism by asserting that any kind of challenge must at some level be ethically suspect, an indication of an opponent's intolerance or prejudice. At its worst, this has seen prohibition rather than discussion, censorship rather than analysis.

The origins of the assumption that history is best studied to be reproached are complex. But a crucial part has been the rise of identity politics as the guiding tool for reading the past. Identity politics— the political issues attending on the complex strands of, among other things, gender, sex, sexuality, class, and ethnicity that comprise an individual's identity—is the offspring of economics and the reinvention of the human being as a consumer. In conjunction with capitalism's creation—intensifying from the nineteenth century onward—of the idea that what matters in the marketplace is the satisfaction of personal taste—"I want x," "I need y"—identity politics has moved into the study of the past because it confirms that what is interesting is what, in history, was done to or for a particular kind of individual, a particular type of identity. This is a species of inquiry dedicated to exploring how the requirements of a specific version of being have been met, or most usually not met: how a particular set of desires and lifestyles has been satisfactorily treated in the past or otherwise.

Identity politics asserted itself in intellectual study in the twentieth century—this is a very rough outline—at first with class. Following Marxist criticism, which has always had more success than Marxism in politics, the treatment of working men became a topic of peculiar interest against what was exposed as the old-fashioned idea that history concerned monarchs and courts rather than fields and factories, generals rather than foot soldiers, leaders rather than followers. The lost voices of working men returned and, for instance, literary texts were mined for how they encoded class oppression and bourgeois attitudes. But Marx, feminism soon pointed out, had been poor at analyzing cultures with women in mind. Marxist criticism was, in turn, revealed as a peculiarly masculinist form of critique. Feminism in the second half of the twentieth century, in particular in the United States and the United Kingdom, aspired—as identity politics continued to grow in importance—to put women back into history and to deplore previous historical interests as chauvinist. In due course, masculinity studies would develop, from the early 1990s, to consider different cultural "styles of masculinity" that could be considered alongside, or sometimes against, the feminist concern with the place of women in history and in the study of history.

Sexuality joined gender: the word "queer" was reclaimed in the late 1980s and 1990s from those who had deployed it as a term of abuse and appropriated for queer studies, which became a name for the academic exploration of the role of gay men, and of gay women, in history. Too long, it was argued, had historical analysis been predicated on heterosexual assumptions and the often tormented history of gay sexuality had been occluded. With sexuality then came race and ethnicity (the extreme liberal arguments about these labels, incidentally, and whether they are somehow racist in themselves, are among the most recent indications of the intersection of moral judgment with identity politics in historical study). The examination of the racially excluded, those marginalized by dominant cultures on the grounds of origin, nationality, or skin color, now could guide the direction of historical inquiry, with its particular interest in the lives of the subaltern (the colonized man or woman, the generalized subject of imperial rule). History was rebuked for its empires while cultural historians and critics were challenged for imperialist views. Likewise, other figures marginalized from centers and previous priorities, inhibited by what are usually conceived as "traditional preoccupations," now attract attention in the steady refining and granulating of identity politics. Incidentally, some liberals think of centers and previous historical priorities as always categories of power, where anything that is dominant is, by definition, oppressive. The only exception, ironically, is the dominance of liberal ideas themselves, which can, it is assumed, never be oppressive.

Identity politics continues to expand its coverage. The mentally ill—sometimes now described in ultraliberal thinking only as victims of a narrow-minded society that categorizes difference as sickness, that exerts power even through diagnosis—have played a part in the expansion of modern disability studies. Such studies, most recently, have regarded the perspective of the physically impaired as well: histories of the deaf or the limbless, for example. Now, too, alongside the establishment of what is now known as Medical Humanities (the general exploration of the places of the diagnosable in historical and contemporary cultures), there is a noticeable rise in the visibility of transgender studies: the once hidden but now recoverable contributions of those for whom biology has not been destiny.

These compound narratives of identity, these strands of inquiry into the past, are important. We need them. But unfortunately they have come at a cost. They have established themselves as of primary or indeed exclusive importance in some areas of intellectual life. The mainstream, the canonical, the enduringly valued, have been reenvisaged as old-fashioned, oppressive, or merely dull. And alongside the development of historical study led by identity politics has arisen a common way of thinking about history and about those concerned with it: as a matter for negative moral judgment.

Identity politics in historical inquiry has, sometimes inadvertently, assured students and scholars that the first and most important way to regard the past is to see it, with the psychoanalysts, as the temporal location of trauma from which we need to recover or have recovered. At its worst, this means that historical investigation is simply a version of finger wagging. Here is an affirmation only of a new strain of Whig history: a reconfirmation of the idea that history is only worth retelling if it is a trajectory upward where what comes next is always more tolerant, better, and morally more acceptable than what happened before. The sense of history's achievements has become, in this, startlingly distorted.

The abuses of slavery, the exploitation of the working classes, the misuse of colonial and imperial power, the problems of those who do not fit into conventional gender categories, the maltreatment of the "Other," the degradation of women, the persecution of homosexuals, the sufferings of the mentally ill, the miserable experience of struggling with trans-sexuality: all have been, and are, prominent topics of post–Second World War liberal historical study. If these have been revealing, they have also helped persuade too many people to regard the past only as something to be glad to be rid of. History is largely visible to such inquiries because of what was not judged right by the standards of the present. Seeking primarily, and sometimes only, for matters that invite disapproval has contaminated our sense that history can offer anything to celebrate other than where it prefigures us. To regard history's attainments, archives and artifacts, largely in terms of their failures or their prophesies has become a marker of how to think analytically about the past.

I'll turn in the final chapter to the specific difficulties that arise in defining local and national identities when the past has been erased or condemned. But here I will remain with more general topics and the troubles blown by the pirrie of modern amnesia and intensified by the compound intellectual invalidation of history and its achievements. The priority of modern identity politics in historical investigation has had effects on how we value and understand what once was done. But it has been equally problematic where the views of others about the past are concerned. Contemporary intellectual priorities have had the consequence of persuading the least intellectually assured of the university educated that what constitutes critical analysis of another person's work or views, what constitutes an appropriate response to another's perceptions, is identifying what is described as morally incorrect about them. Analysis can, here (and I am talking of extreme cases), be diminished into a search for what are classified as another person's hidden assumptions that are not ethically acceptable. Students and scholars have become highly trained to spot what they deem as heresy in a regulated system of thought that demarcates as much as it demands the orthodox. (And being "nonjudgmental" has strangely become, as many have recognized, a virtue: not having an opinion on lifestyles, values, and principles is the new opinion.)

One consequence of the concomitant assumption that what is important in history is only that which prefigures modern liberal values is that any other concern with the archives of the past has been trivialized. In order to cope with the interpretive preference for what is bad in history, anything else, any other form of approach, has—in the most problematic and least robust areas of intellectual life—been made acceptable by being made bland. This is true in some strands of popular culture and in the more general mental fallout from poststructuralism. But it is also now dispiritingly true of a widespread popular understanding of what an education in the arts and humanities is.

To put this point in an apparently bizarre way, trivialization is most obvious—though it may not appear initially so—in the transformation of the study of art, literature, history, music, politics, culture, or place, into topics that are taught for assessment. And, more importantly, into assessment that is regulated by assessment criteria. The well-intentioned has had injurious outcomes, however much the principle of *abusus non tollit usum* might be claimed to obtain. Such criteria are the new ways in which irregularity in a knowledge of history is constructed: they are effective, too, in contributing to how attitudes to pasts are formed and analysis of them managed. Of course, the logic of assessment criteria needs no justification in theory. They are about consistency and clarity. But, all the same, these criteria contribute influentially to the metamorphosis of the achievements of the past into something instrumental to the present. Such criteria belong within a broader contemporary Western understanding of education, particularly at school but increasingly in the universities, as sparely functional, as defined by targets and map-able achievements, by grades and numbers. They are part of the assumption that education is an episode in a "development plan" for a child or young person, necessary for their transformation into an employee. A good grade, marked fairly and transparently against detailed and publicly accessible assessment criteria achieved by a student taught to write *to* the assessment criteria, is now the key educational ambition.

Assessment criteria do many things for a variety disciplines. Scientists, mathematicians, engineers, and medical faculty are concerned about them, I know. But in this book about the loss of the past it is how they inflect, and infect, our knowledge of history that bothers me. Such criteria determine what that knowledge must look like. At high school, as the phrase goes, boxes must be ticked. It is not a metaphor. This number of texts discussed, that number of points per paragraph, this indication of "empathy," that ability to refer to "historical context," this evidence of an understanding of irony, that evidence of an ability to read a source. Through the formal structures of education, what students learn is what can be graded according to a published set of requirements about what is acceptable, and necessary, to say. Most of what is valued—there are extreme cases of *all* that is valued—is what can have a numerical value assigned to it in accordance with its coherence to a checklist. Sometimes, for instance in the International Baccalaureate (IB), the requirements are of exceptional precision. Because the IB is marked internationally, the assessment criteria have to be peculiarly exact to ensure that a marker on one side of the world can be seen transparently to have done the same job as a marker on the other, to have produced results consistent with everyone else. Admirable in intention, these requirements for what writing about the past looks like are flattening, requiring teachers to a remarkably extended degree to "teach to the test."

What was once discussion of ideas, of writing or speaking, is now being replaced by "feedback." This is the response—often bureaucratized with documents, in-house web procedures, and word counts—of the grader or evaluator to a piece of work or an oral presentation. It is the official explanation of how a student's achievement conformed or did not conform to the criteria for assessment. At the starting point of all of this are unobjectionable commitments: justice and equity, clarity and consistency. But the consequences have proved a cause for regret because the past has been translated into a narrowly defined test and the academic response to the test has been regulated to an extreme degree about what can and cannot be said.

Historical knowledge in its broadest sense comes to the young as a matter on which to be assessed and/or in which to find evidence that things have improved, or need to improve. There are some attempts to make history a little more than this, though they are only on the present's terms and understood in the least demanding of ways. Among other frames of reference through which pupils are taught to comprehend historical achievement—again, in multiple forms—is the language of "relevance" and "empathy," and, a word that is currently establishing itself in educational documents in England, that which is "relatable." That last term appeared initially, says *OED*, in its contemporary sense in a schoolteaching manual in 1965. Each of these concepts assumes that the past is of value only so long as it directly and seemingly transparently can be thought to "relate" to the present moment, and, as often as not, the needs and feelings of a particular individual in that moment. Each is a term, despite its apparent resistance to modernity's normative habits of mind, produced by an economic culture that prefers when the past matches, and pleases, the

current requirements of its consumer. They turn historical achievement into that familiar category of the contemporary world of markets and advertisers: something that, potentially, can "satisfy."

None of those terms, of "empathy," "relevance," "relatable," is
intrinsically mistaken. They are the unsteady results of what remains
of an ambition to make connections with history, to understand the
past and, in a manner of speaking, to feel with it. A relationship with
history is exactly that for which *Forgetfulness*, in its usually pejorist
convictions, recognizes we have lost. Yet the trouble with these ideas,
circulating through contemporary education, is that they are nomi-
nal in ambition and presentist in conception. They propose, as I have
said, that the past is primarily of interest only if it is not really the past.
They require that history speaks directly and uncomplicatedly to the
current moment, or that—in the notion of empathy—its artifacts are
comprehensible only when they are emotionally identical to what is
wanted now. There is, by the way, a debate to be had about whether
there can ever be such a thing as "empathy:" a word that originally
meant in psychology, as *OED* expresses it, "The quality or power of
projecting one's personality into or mentally identifying oneself with
an object of contemplation, and so fully understanding or appreciat-
ing it." It is possible to sympathize, yes. But is it, ever, epistemolog-
ically, realistic to think we could do something more absolute than
that: that we could *fully* understand?

At its worst, where the relationship to history is concerned, we
are advising pupils and students that if they do not immediately
find something "relatable" then it must go. And in that sense of the
"immediate" is another modern challenge for the survival of history
amid the world we have created for ourselves. Obtaining knowledge
of the past and endeavoring to understand it is effortful. The business
of comprehending something from days long gone requires time and
labor: reading, traveling, looking, thinking. And as even the English

literary critic Sir Frank Kermode (1919–2010) recognized, many of us would rather do anything than read. Such strenuous acquisition of knowledge and the hard-thinking establishment of ideas do not easily fit into an entitlement culture. In the simple privileging of the "now" and the "next"—in education and beyond—and in the expectation that the consumer can have what he or she desires more or less straightaway, difficult-to-obtain knowledge of history, and sufficient understanding of that knowledge, is made peculiarly unappealing.

In a consumerist environment promising its members that what satisfies is what others must provide, educators train a generation denied much real understanding of intellectual responsibility, the nature of effort, and the chance of knowing that there are things more complex than that which merely gratifies now (assuming for a moment that the gratification of instant obtainment really is gratification). And then, finally, in universities in the United Kingdom, we are asked by the government to confirm to our students at the end of their education, in accordance with the values of the National Student Survey (NSS), that the highest goal of an intellectual exploration of the past is derived from *satis*, the Latin for "enough," and *facere*, "to do." "It was enough," perhaps, is enough—or at least having been given what one had expected. The gold measure of the government-sanctioned soon-to-be-graduates' assessment of a university education (the NSS was launched in 2005) is now the question: "did it satisfy you?" The policy makers have, that is to say, diminished an exploration of the archives and achievements of history (indeed, intellectual exploration in all disciplines in general) into the blandest of consumerist activities. The aim is apparently identical to making sure the customer liked the cup of coffee.

This book began in ancient Mycenae. But now it reaches rather less ancient Athens. Mycenae was emblematically useful as a point from which to compare the modern world's conception of time and memory so that its features stood out with clarity. Yet, turning to the Socratic tradition, beginning in the ancient capital of the Hellenic world, it is possible to make another comparison: to discern a practice of mind that is not a commonplace within our current understanding of thought and the nature of teaching. Socratic thinking, that is to say, involved a conception of education—and equally of daily mental life—which was defined by strenuousness and critical integrity; by its readiness, as W. H. Auden would say, to ask the hard question.

The Athenian philosopher Socrates (470/69–399 BC) had faith, as was to be expected, in his own *polis*, and in the gods and traditions that involved. This faith may have cost him his life. Socrates as an old man had little sympathy with the new Athenian government, and he championed Sparta as a preferable culture while rebuking Athenian political decline. For better or for worse, the philosopher would not retract his criticisms and the result was fatal. Socrates left nothing in writing. As the central figure of Western ethical philosophy, Socrates is presence and absence, body and ghost. He exists to subsequent minds only through the memories of others. In a forgetfulness culture, he might have been lost. But he was remembered in the writing of two of his most celebrated pupils: Plato (428/7 or 424/3–348/7 BC), who employed the figure of "Socrates" as the teacher in his philosophical dialogues, and the historian Xenophon (c.430–354 BC), whose *Memorabilia* (c.371 BC) contains recollections and explanations of Socrates's thinking.

Socrates, it goes without saying, did not regard the intellectual life as anything to do with tests or market satisfaction. He was a stranger to grades and examination criteria. But he was not a stranger to principle. The life of the mind was for him, we learn from those he taught, about being fully human, and being both reasonable and fair. Philosophy for this, by all accounts, rather ugly and physically charmless man, was practiced in questioning. (And, incidentally, that questioning was decisively oral: conversation and dialogue were for Socrates the highest form of teaching and learning. The absence of written work is not, I think, a sign of idleness, accident, or lack of commitment but, on the contrary, the result of a conviction.)

A questioning reason, as Socrates perceived it, was the central requirement for becoming wise and sensible. Answering queries prompted the mind to work. It cultivated logic and intelligence. And to an answer, Socrates, we gather from his pupils, always posed another inquiry, probing the strength of the previous reasoning. After the answer to that question, he constructed another … and another. Socrates made a career, it might be said, by asking variants of the same inquiry: "Is that entirely true?" "Is that entirely principled?" "Is that entirely just?" The mind, this ancient Greek thought, was sharpened rather than overwhelmed by such persistence: the speaker was obliged to examine his or her assumptions and to consider other perspectives as well as to identify insecure reasoning or overlooked implications.

Socrates's own earnest concern, as he paced the streets of Athens chatting, we are told, to anyone he met, was how to live a good life. He interested himself little in politics—and his political naïveté might, as I said, have cost him his life. Yet virtuous practice in the day-to-day was Socrates's primary topic. He was a philosopher-in-ordinary more than a court sage. Where was virtue to be found in daily life, he inquired? Pursuing the theme that was a preoccupation of Athenian ethics generally, Socrates inspired his listeners, said Xenophon in the *Memorabilia*, "with a desire for goodness and [offered] them hope that, if they took themselves in hand, they would become truly good." Socrates's charisma persuaded men and women to consider what the Judeo-Christian tradition would call righteousness, and to consider too the belief that the citizen's first duty was to think rationally and to retain integrity in thought and behavior.

The Socratic conception of intellectual development was of something sincerely but not narrowly "useful." Philosophy was for the streets and kitchens, for the shops and temples: its vitality came from the fact that it addressed lived experience rather than the abstract or abstracted. And this thinking was fearless. Philosophy's central obligation, as Socrates perceived it, was to train the mind to analyze that which mattered in the belief that only the reasonable could be justified, and only that which had been intellectually examined could be supportable. He tells us, that is to say, that there is an ethical responsibility, a moral requirement, to discuss without merely passive acceptance of the received, the authoritarian, or the confined. What was not reasonable—the mere imposition of authority, of popular or political opinion, of mere orthodoxies that are accepted because they are orthodoxies, or the sanction solely of precedent—could not be credible on its own.

To the rational discovery of right principle, or, in the modern sense, simply the discovering of an adequate understanding of what is happening and an evaluation of it, this printless philosopher dedicated his formidable interrogative powers. Socrates, uncompromising examiner of what is being said and what it means, is an ancient ideal to remember when evaluating the nature of modern forgetfulness and what it is doing to us. As our education systems turn the past into something to dislike, trivialize, or to be examined on, intellectuals and policy makers assist in the modern world's more general dismissal and downplaying of history. The ancient voice of Socrates would require from us all a more rigorous understanding of what we are doing, what it means, and what its outcomes might be for our world and those who will inherit it. Socrates's ancient culture—the citizens of the Hellenic *polis*—valued the noble deeds and great achievements of long ago. Remaining Homeric, that culture comprehended that there was worth in continuities and in memory. Plato's teacher would certainly have wanted to know whether we, at the beginning of the twenty-first century, had adequately understood the implications of, instead, making forgetting the principal attitude to the past.

6

The problems of forgetting national and local histories

"How is your doom revers'd, which eas'd my care
When Troy was ruin'd in that cruel war?"

VERGIL, *Aeneid*, Book 1, trans. John Dryden

The English political philosopher, Thomas Hobbes (1588–1679), was an apologist for the Divine Right of Kings in an age of Civil War. In his, for many, notorious book on the social contract, *Leviathan, or The Matter, Forme and Power of a Common Wealth Ecclesiasticall and Civil* (1651), Hobbes expressed his gloomy, but also gravely optimistic, vision of humanity in a state of nature. He proposed that human beings who were not governed by strong regulations and strong leaders were condemned to a permanent condition of mutual strife. His ideas are part of the modern foundation, though much modified, of Conservative thinking about the requirement for law, order, moral clarity, and the durable structures of family and state. Once a society lost its absolute monarch, as Hobbes put it, there is "a returne to Confusion, and to the condition of a War of every man against every man." That is an echo of Macduff, in Shakespeare's *Macbeth* (1611), who declares that "boundless intemperance | In nature is a tyranny" (Act 4, sc. 3, ll. 67–8).

Hobbes was a theorist of the conditions of confusion not only politically but also mentally. He was a ruminator on psychological blanks and losses, a conceptualizer of forgetting (including forgetting the need for kings). Where political turmoil could be halted by a monarch who implemented anything but moral relativism, nothing, for Hobbes, could, alas, forestall the fading of the past. Hobbes's governing metaphor for memory loss was a long slow journey both in time and space away from a once familiar city. The further a traveler moved geographically and chronologically from that location, the less was visible, as well as recollectable, of an urban environment previously known. On a walk beyond them, cities became merely towers and spires, then faint masses on the horizon, then lost altogether. That was comparable to the process of endeavoring to recall the same city when memory was fading. Losing sight of a particular location, forgetting its shape and its nature, was Hobbes's chief model for mental bereavement, for the homelessness and figurative statelessness brought about by forgetting. After "a great distance of time," a man's memory of the past, Hobbes said, "is weak; and we lose of Cities we have seen, many particular Streets." Forgetting for Hobbes was bound up with the abandonment of location, with the fading sense of a place we used to know.

Walking away in *Leviathan*—Hobbes, as it happens, died after a paralytic stroke had taken away both his memory and his ability to walk—was a figure for memory loss and all the dissolution that implied. Migration, I could say, was his metaphorical representation of disappearing familiarities, faltering bonds, and growing blankness without a home. This last chapter is about these topics: about migration and the erosion of security, the loss of tradition and history that is involved not so much for the migrant—about whom we know much—but, potentially, the host. The conjunction of this challenge with the homogenizing forces of a global capitalism, which has rendered experience in multiple towns and cities simply repeatable, has intensified a contemporary sense of lost specificity. Such homogenization has further eroded our comprehension of the specialness of urban spaces, collapsing the distinctive local into that which could be more or less anywhere. My final chapter has no adequate understanding of the political or intellectual way ahead. It claims, rather, that the best that is available to the present is a chance to clarify the difficulties involved in finding such ways.

I start by examining a localized and relatively minor form of historical experience: the relationship between memory and place in post-Romantic writing about the natural world. I investigate a cluster of writers from the nineteenth century to the present who have been looking for connections with their own lands by literally looking at the—land. What concerns me here is the recent (i.e., in the last 200 years) interest in recovering or sometimes imagining an ancient idea of belonging. Here is a consideration of those who have probed the antique issue of what home could look like when history is remembered (or at least believed to be remembered). The writers who mull over these topics are, I suggest, dimly searching for the values of Homeric epic understood as rootedness in continuations and the bonding such continuations create. I hold these writers as symptomatic: they are not models uncritically to follow or proposals simply to accept. They are evidence, rather, of a need. My discussion leads me to the major contemporary issue of national and cultural pasts in relation to the implications of internationalization in Western communities. My theme here is the challenge of global capitalism and of contemporary migration—and the challenge of how such migration can be discussed. The argument is that we have deprived ourselves both of the tools and the discursive space in which to examine the potential consequences of these cultural, economic, and political topics adequately. What we can know is simply that we don't know what will happen. Both by diminishing the place of history in our lives in general and by limiting discussion, except in specific terms, of whether certain forms of localized history relate to home, we have denied ourselves most ways, except extreme ones, of envisaging how the future relates in any way to what once happened.

*   *   *

The seventeenth and eighteenth centuries had their antiquarians who occasionally interested themselves in the historical artifacts of the European countryside. The extraordinary prehistoric chamber of Newgrange in County Meath, Ireland, for instance, was first explored by antiquarians shortly after it was rediscovered in 1699 by accidental agricultural digging. That was not unique. Stonehenge, the most famous prehistoric site in England, has never been lost—King Henry VIII (1491–1547) knew enough about it to put it up for sale (commodifying history has never been only a modern phenomenon). But it was in the nineteenth century, the beginning of modernity, that the serious development of prehistoric field studies properly began ("prehistoric," the word, dates from 1832). Field clubs, archaeological societies, and privately supported individuals particularly in Northern Europe did much to explore, and occasionally to damage, the barrows, tumuli, grave mounds, megaliths, cairns, and buried bones of the undocumented past. When Dr. Mortimer in Arthur Conan Doyle's detective novel of ancestry and inheritance, *The Hound of the Baskervilles* (1902), lunches with Dr. Watson and Sir Henry Baskerville, Mortimer, we learn, has been "excavating a barrow at Long Down and has got a prehistoric skull which fills him with great joy." His real-life counterparts were doing the same.

Comprehending the countryside as ancient, as once the habitation of long dead generations, produced a new mode in the nineteenth and twentieth centuries for perceiving or at least fantasizing what of the past survived beyond cities and towns, villages, and hamlets. A counterbalancing to the preference of capitalism for tomorrow, the exposition of rural antiquity—an antiquity far more recent than the fossils but still greatly beyond the stretch of human memory—put a modest weight in the other tray of the scales. "We sometimes feel," said the Argentinean-born naturalist William Henry Hudson (1841–1922) in *Hampshire Days* (1903), "a kinship with, and are strangely drawn to the dead, the long long dead, the men who knew not life in towns, and felt no strangeness in sun and wind and rain." It was a faintly Homeric desire for kinship with those who had lived differently many centuries ago that required, as far as Hudson was concerned, neither apology nor *apologia*. The apprehension of a fragile connection with, at least a curiosity about, the long long dead was enough. That imprecise but felt attraction back through lands and centuries, that cloudy sense of affinity with exceptionally different worlds, was the faded trace of a need to be grounded in a location that was not alienated by time.

There is a similar impulse, and similar imprecision, in Thomas Hardy's poem about the reach of the past, "In the Old Theatre, Fiesole (April 1887)":

I traced the Circus whose gray stones incline
Where Rome and dim Etruria interjoin,
Till came a child who showed an ancient coin
That bore the image of a Constantine.

She lightly passed; nor did she once opine
How, better than all books, she had raised for me
In swift perspective Europe's history
Through the vast years of Caesar's sceptred line.

For in my distant plot of English loam
'Twas but to delve, and straightway there to find
Coins of like impress. As with one half blind
Whom common simples cure, her act flashed home
In that mute moment to my opened mind
The power, the pride, the reach of perished Rome.

Hardy's poem leaves his experience unanalyzed. The words permit the reader to ponder the ending of empires and might, perhaps, invite thought on the durability of the British Empire, about which the poet was doubtful. Yet there is also an ineffability—a hard-to-articulate wonder in the middle of a forgetful modernity about the lost ubiquity of Rome that had stretched far into England, Scotland, and Wales until the beginning of the fifth century. Hardy's text conjures a felt union with an ancient but still fractionally knowable time, a sense of the antiquity of his own "English loam" and its complex history, involved with other places while being itself.

The English photographer and nature walker Alfred Watkins (1855–1935) began his remarkable book, *The Old Straight Track* (1925), by quoting those same words of W. H. Hudson about kinships. Watkins, an important late Victorian figure in the changing sense of how to read English lands through time, searched out what he thought were the deepest identities of place and contextualized modern England as one profoundly organized by its past, proposing that its landscapes were a repository of ancient memory.

For Watkins, initially pacing the fields and hills of Herefordshire, then, afterward, more widely in Great Britain, there seemed irrefutable evidence that pre-Roman inhabitants of the British Isles had an involved but planned system of navigation. They had divided up topography into lines. Those inhabitants, Watkins proposed, had created a network of crossings that traversed the countryside, aligned with the sun or motion of a star, and marking out the landscape with course after course. Partially recoverable by an investigation of mounds, beacons, megaliths, earthworks, barrows, and known sites of pagan worship, the exact purpose of the so-called leys—Watkins thought this was an ancient word for "tracks"—was lost. The lines might have marked trade routes or they might have been ceremonial paths. No one knew. Watkins, certainly, had no sense that the ley lines, as later New Age disciples would claim, were channels of the earth's power and had spiritual or creative force. He was concerned with what he thought hard, rational topographical evidence, not with what he would no doubt have regarded as moonshine. "[We] crave to know more of the life and doings of the people who lived in Britain before the Romans came," Watkins said in the same spirit as W. H. Hudson. In the organization of specific forms of local and national landscape he found some satisfaction to that craving, discovering solid evidence, so he believed, of pasts almost too remote to conceive.

The landscape—I am concentrating on British landscape but this is not meant to be a way of seeing peculiar to any one area—was being perceived as an archive of histories that had been nearly forgotten. Walking among the hills and fields emerged, in turn, as a noticeable twentieth-century practice—with its origins in the nineteenth—for calling to mind those pasts that were almost, but not completely, gone. Such walking became a mode of locomotion that enabled men and women to attend to what did still remain, even if only in the imagination, of remote times. Here were delicate explorations of spectral but distinctive identities of places-with-a-history, discoverable through the remaining presence of what had once occurred there. "Walking," says Rebecca Solnit in her *Wanderlust: A History of Walking* (2000), "shares with making and working that crucial element of engagement of the body and the mind with the world, of knowing the world through the body and the body through the world." This is specifically true of walking in ancient or ancestral landscapes, which for a while has become the far-flung successor, several thousand years later, to a memory culture's devotion to the past.

Ordnance Survey, the leading British map-makers, have added prehistoric and Roman features to their cartographic key ("site of antiquity," "visible earthwork"), enabling a walker to read maps as charts that expose a little of how things used to be. It is possible, now, even to exclude the present altogether with the *Ordnance Survey Map of Ancient Britain*, first printed in 1964. The *Ordnance Survey Map of Roman Britain* is—with pleasing counterfactuality—earlier: its first edition was published in 1924, some half a century before the redis-covery of the paradigm-shifting Roman remains at Fishbourne, in West Sussex, which strongly suggested the Italian occupiers had been welcomed by existing power structures: that the "invasion" had been more of a merger. The Romans' mark, as Hardy knew, remains. The British journalist Charlotte Higgins knows it too. With a guide and a map, as well as a Classics degree from the University of Oxford, Higgins walked Caesar's northern territories for her *Under Another Sky: Journeys in Roman Britain* (2013), recording what it felt like to envisage on location the not entirely vanished landscape of nearly two millennia previously. Looking for what "Britain" felt like "under another sky," Higgins aspired to explore, she said,

> what this period means, and has meant to a British sense of his-tory and identity. I wanted to discover the ways in which the idea of Roman Britain has resonated in British culture and still forms part of the texture of its landscapes—not just through the sublime contours of the Northumberland hills, but in humbler urban and suburban tracts of territory.

In the disposition of land, the outlines of far-gone peoples— literate, preliterate, and those whose literary remains have almost completely vanished—are still presences, Higgins ventures, which, however inexactly, still mean. Faintly perceptible, palely imaginable through antiquity's mists and rime, through the occasional evidence of a darker patch of soil here or a stone laid on top of another there, is something for Higgins like a cultural memory, a chance for human beings to remain dimly in touch with what happened before.

Landscape, for those seeking in space a different relationship to time, has become like a page in an epic. Schliemann the archeologist would have recognized this: an ambition to discover in what lingers on and below ground the hard evidence of remote pasts. Here is a slight but still decipherable compendium of heroic—as well as unheroic—deeds that have nearly disappeared, but not quite. And those that remain on the cusp of remembrance, men and women who are almost forgotten but not entirely, are of value to the epics of the ancient Mediterranean themselves. For those great poems created room to recollect and honor the specters of specters. The narratives of the deeds of Odysseus, Achilles, Agamemnon, Hector, and the gods were, for Homer, part of a collective possession. In epic was an immense act of resistance to forgetfulness that was a shared possession even as "Homer" himself was no single man. His name was a placeholder for a habit of human recollection; his words, as Adam Nicolson phrases it, "are the descendants of memory and power." Yet this memory was not only for heroic achievements that could be narrated at length. It was for the tiniest memories of the long gone too: individuals on the very edges of Lethe.

Antinous in Book 2 of the *Odyssey* rebukes Telemachus, Odysseus's son, over the wiles of his, Telemachus's, mother, Penelope. Antinous is vexed about her continuing entertainment of suitors at home in Ithaca. It is unseemly, disloyal, and disruptive. In Antinous's speech of chastisement—Penelope must decide rather than flirt—the reader momentarily learns the names of three women from, we must assume, the furthest roots of Greek memory:

> But if [Penelope] shall continue for long to vex the sons of the Achaeans, possessing in her mind those advantages with which Athene has endowed her above other women, knowledge of beautiful handiwork, and good sense, and cleverness, such as we have never yet heard that any of the women of old knew, those fair-tressed Achaean women who lived long ago, Tyro and Alcemene and Mycene of the fair crown—of whom not one was like Penelope in shrewd device[.]

Who were Tyro, Alcemene, and Mycene? We gather names: Antinous speaks as if his listeners will recognize them as part of the inherited corpus of knowledge linking the present back to an undatable past. We know that they had beautiful hair. We know that they were experts at needlework, though not so gifted as the wife of Odysseus. We know that they were clever. And that is all. Yet it is something. Tyro, Alcemene, and Mycene attend on us faintly still.

The ghostly figures of almost vanished lives have been imagined in the epic pages, the Homeric leaves, of the countryside too. "The English landscape," said the British academic historian W. G. Hoskins (1908–92) in his widely read book, *The Making of the English Landscape* (1955), "to those who know how to read it aright, is the richest historical record we possess." This was a volume that helped create the notion of "local history"—Hoskins established the first university department for that new academic discipline at what is now the University of Leicester. So doing, he helped place, for a while, the idea of the legibility of landscape as a witness to, and embodiment of, the far remote past in the modern education system. Reading the meaning of antique lands contributed—in felt and imaginative terms—to an understanding, as Hoskins described it, of local identity.

And even when the past was not *that* remote, the ground still bore its marks that were worthy of attention. Bronze Age outworks are not to be found everywhere. "But most of England," Hoskins told his readers, "is 1,000 years old, and in a walk of a few miles one can touch nearly every century in that long stretch of time." The same could be said, of course, of many landscapes other than the English. But the point, for Hoskins, was about discerning (however provisionally) the identity of locality as it was marked by the passage of time.

A significant strand of modern nature writing welcomes a gently countercultural assertion of continuities. It has proved a literary practice that modestly returns the body and mind to a relationship with pasts in a modernity that generally desires the opposite. Remote locations, hidden privacies, have acquired the charm of being far from busy cities. But they also possess the aura of seemingly lost ways of existing. The English environmentalist Roger Deakin (1943–2006), writing in his beautiful, posthumously published book, *Wildwood: A Journey through Trees* (2007), offers a tribute to the secluded arboreal and what he sees as its relationship with the clock and calendar. "Woods, like water," Deakin says,

> have been suppressed by motorways and the modern world, and have come to look like the subconscious of the landscape. They have become the guardians of our dreams of greenwood liberty, of our wildwood, feral, childhood selves, of Richmal Crompton's Just William and his outlaws. They hold the merriness of Merry England, of yew longbows, of Robin Hood and his outlaw band. But they are also repositories of the ancient stories, of the Icelandic myths of Ygdrasil the Tree of Life, Robert Graves's "The Battle of the Trees" and the myths of Sir James Frazer's *Golden Bough*. The enemies of woods are always the enemies of culture and humanity.

Trees emerge here as a way of remembering themselves; of, how-ever fancifully and sentimentally, remaining in contact with what are framed as local identities. Modernity's courtship of tomorrow has compelled the construction of idealized pasts that can seemingly be contacted primarily by intuition. Where we cannot remember, we can—Deakin invites us—dream.

Wildness has been for the metropolitan psycho-geographers—Iain Sinclair in *London Orbital: A Walk Around the M25* (2002); Paul Farley and Michael Symmons Roberts in *Edgelands: Journeys into England's True Wilderness* (2011); Nick Papadimitriou in *Scarp* (2012), for instance—rediscovered in the feral. Yet more familiar forms of wil-derness are turned into narrative because they are out of the feral, further from the scenes of modernity's existence and its abandoned, perishing sites. The imagined connections to histories and that which is beyond modern time may, in this writing, be whimsical, gushing, or odd. Yet what is important for my purpose is not so much to eval-uate the texts but to observe the import of their existence. For here is another outfall of a fugitive hope for reconnection with history. Here are feelings and acts of invention that are symptoms of, and clues to, the ache modernity leaves us, the experience of being out of place because dislocated from decent knowledge of pasts we can compre-hend as part of our own.

"Anyone who lives in a city," says the literary academic and wanderer, Robert Macfarlane, phrasing the simplest version of the antimodern impulse in *The Wild Places* (2007), "will know the feeling of having been there too long." Out in the woods and fields, and espe-cially along the ancient tracks—what Macfarlane follows in *The Old Ways: A Journey on Foot* (2012)—modern connections with landscape revitalize the vocabulary of affiliations and of the peculiar pleasures of wildness as spaces outside the present. It has recently been possible in England even to write a history of the weather, an affirmation that what is breathed and felt on the skin has a human history. Alexandra Harris in *Weatherland: Writers and Artists under English Skies* (2015) invites her reader to comprehend, amid northern dampness and chills, generations of artists and writers recording what being out in the elements feels like. Those walking in England can experience the past according to what the skies are doing.

The aspirations for felt history, sometimes for history literally underfoot or in the air, seek the relief from modernity that the anfractuous, the circuitous, the perambulatory permits. Sometimes, what has been manifested is a head-on examination of what home might look like, the most obvious concept for an identity grounded in space and time. Traveling around a land raises questions about belonging that are not merely spatial but abstract—and also about what it means to be without security. "Like being married," says the Shetland singer and writer Mallachy Tallack in *Sixty Degrees North: Around the World in Search of Home* (2015),

> being at home is not a passive state. It is a process, in which the heart must be engaged. That is as true for the reindeer herders of Siberia, whose home may be hundreds of square miles, as it is for the inhabitants of a tiny village on a tiny island. For many people this is not so. Home for them is nowhere in particular. It is the house in which their belongings are kept and in which they go to sleep at night. It extends no further than that. This is the condition of our time. It is a marriage without love, a relationship without commitment. And it is, surely, a kind of homelessness.

Sixty Degrees North is literally a postbereavement history—retelling a journey across all the territories on the 60° line of longitude in search of something, after loss, which is and is not a physical place. Tallack, whose music includes "Leaving My Old Self Behind" (2013), narrates a secular pilgrimage to a secular shrine, both to escape who he is and find it. The location of this shrine is not immediately apparent. But the journey is hopeful. Writing about a quest for personal refuge as a conflict with estrangement, Tallack produces a book reaching in words toward a more-than-personal shelter and for a place that feels like an achieved stability.

Wildness and belonging, particularly amid landscapes that are outwardly aloof from modern time, prove topics of some of the most revealingly alternative of contemporary books about the natural world. The British archeologist Francis Pryor thinks that the study of prehistory takes you into cultures that thought more steadily about the present moment than about the next, and which were devoted to the ongoing nature of the family as a center of being and the source of home. Here, again, we are back with the remotest predecessors of Mycenae. "In today's fast-paced urban world," Pryor observes in his informal book, *Home: A Time Traveller's Tales from Britain's Prehistory* (2014), "it's all about achievement and potential 'going forward'. We seem to be losing sight of our daily lives in the here and now." Secure daily life is what he claims true of ancient cultures over whose remains the grasses have grown. Prehistoric traces, once assembled and interpreted, reveal communities, Pryor declares, which were at ease with themselves, bounded with each other through family traditions rather than preoccupied by unknown vistas of speculative possibility. Whether this is entirely true or not of prehistory no one can be sure. But that is less important than recognizing the forces that create a desire to believe it.

Other authors of blazons to local topography, musing on the marks of ancient people and historical ways of life, celebrate landscapes and natural forms, yet are mournful of their vulnerability—their capacity to be brought unwillingly into an inhospitable modernity. The author and farmer John Lewis-Stempel, whose family has inhabited the same county farm for more than 700 years, writes in *Meadowland: The*

Private Life of an English Field (2014), of a different world. He speaks of a sense of accommodation to barely conceivable histories that darkness in rural Herefordshire reveals—by coincidence where Alfred Watkins had begun tracking his ley lines—just as he finds in the old technique for making hay (with a scythe instead of a machine) an unexpected satisfaction. "To stand in an immense starred night is to be a citizen of the universe," Lewis-Stempel remarks rhapsodically. "London has not seen the stars since the Blitz." Yet this mode of anti-modern, antiurban visuality, as Lewis-Stempel knows, is precarious. "This is a dying world," he adds fiercely. "A nearby farm is diversifying into holiday accommodation. Their field of beautiful aspect will grow tipis. Which is like a dog shitting on a white Berber carpet."

The Scottish poet Kathleen Jamie writes of the out-of-the-way that is a kind of real but wild home too: the rare Scottish birds of prey, the shy mammal both aquatic and terrene, the peculiar patterns of Highland rain, the elusive gannet's skull that she hopes to discover one day on the remotest stretches of the west coast. Even in its title, Jamie's collection of essays, *Findings* (2005), encapsulates the plea-sures of random discovery abutted by an idea of secular revelation, a recovery of lost correlations. And seemingly untamed Scotland finds another exponent in the hill-walker and writer Mike Cawthorne's *Wild Voices: Journeys through Time in the Scottish Highlands* (2014). There too, like John Lewis-Stempel in Herefordshire, is a lament for, as well as a celebration of, locations outside a contemporary understanding of what is important about chronology. Cawthorne understands that wild nature, marked by human history but detached from modernity for the moment, is up for sale. "We have this treeless waste, which in a way I love, of course," he says, thinking of how the Highlands look after the Clearances, "and would hate to see it covered in turbines and dams, but it used to be so much richer." It is a simple line. But it means that even connections to local wild spaces are inside, as well as outside, history: in danger of being pulled into, and dissolved by, the present.

"Wood cuts most easily across its age-rings, against time," observes the English travel writer and historian of exiles, Philip Marsden in *Rising Ground: A Search for the Spirit of Place* (2014), "while the stone breaks in the way it was made. It is as if the binding of living things must be stronger than time, so brief is their existence. Stone, on the other hand, grows not in years and decades, but in thousands of years. It has no urgency." Marsden can do almost nothing against modernity and its focused determination to regard primarily the future. But he can, like some other contemporary nature writers, fashion in language a temporary alternative. Inviting a different form of attention to the passage of years than that which we habitually comprehend, Marsden's eloquent sentences pause over the strength that ages confer in a poetic assimilation of identity, history, and durability.

Marsden is a troubadour of what he calls the "spirit of place" as well as, appropriately, a historian of the displaced. There is a correspondence for him between human beings rummaging in the ruins of what used to be home and the walker's experience of felt belonging in natural landscapes. Marsden's fictionalized *The Bronski House: A Return to the Borderlands* (1995) narrates, for example, in inventive literary form, the destruction of the old ways of life in eastern Poland with the arrival of the Red Army in 1939. It is an elegy for a country that was not, like stone, permitted to grow but was wrecked by Soviet ambition. More extensively, Marsden's *The Crossing Place: A Journey among the Armenians* (1993) recounts his own search, from Jerusalem and Venice to the *fedayi* of Yerevan (militia fighting against the Russians and Turks) for the surviving heart of Armenia. So doing, Marsden analyses the cultural and political history of the Armenians, from the establishment of the Kingdom of Van in 860 BC to the present day. An ancient people, the builders of one of the great civilizations of Europe and the Near East, the Armenians have a long history of anguish, most recently in the events of the 1915 genocide and the continuing repudiation of Armenian culture by neighboring states. Yet violence and destruction have never quite extinguished them. Armenia's modern history has been one of exile, of dispossession and attempts to maintain ways of life across boundaries. But they survive still, retaining cultural memory. "It was what they knew of the world," Marsden says of his attraction to Armenians, musing on his fascination with an indestructible people, "of the deep lessons of loss and landlessness, of living among strangers, of how to make light of borders and the obstacles of long journeys." His journey involves, as it did in *Rising Ground*, a consideration of what is conceptually as well as physically home. Marsden seeks out the places—remote, sometimes literally embattled—where the ancient Armenian traditions are still alive. *The Crossing Place*, studying "all the inherited fear of lost land," is about a resistance to forgetting, about the preservation of a long-ago established but bravely continuing culture.

Migration—chosen, necessitated, or forced—is no stranger to human history and particularly in modern Europe and North America. *Homo sapiens* is unique as a species alive on the planet today in its ability to choose to move—and in its simple ability *to* move. Earth's occupation by people is a function of this nomadic capability since no other living creature has willed its departure from one climate to another, from one land mass to a different one, let alone made the resettlement work. A single person's DNA in the West can bear traces of compound ethnic origins, a glimpse of biological borders crossed in forgotten as well as, sometimes, remembered time. Those of us with known compound heritage—mine from Irish, English, and Hungarian families within the last century—understand a corporeal version of this specific and literal bind to the decisions and necessities of the past.

But does the compound nature of an individual's inheritance work unproblematically as a model for cultures as a whole? Forced migration, compelled displacement (not least those of the Armenians), is part of the tortured past of Europe during and immediately after the Second World War. This is a history that modernity has not, for obvious reasons, forgotten. But the memories bring difficulties. And those have become peculiarly clear in responses to recent patterns in Western demography. During the twentieth century, there has been a change in the direction of European migration. The net migratory *deficit* for Europe between the years 1920 and 1940, as the Italian professor of demography Massimo Livi-Bacci points out, "amounted to 7 million, and for 1950–70 about 4 million." Europe had been losing its population—because of fascism, postconflict austerity, and post-victory reorganization of national borders. But then the flow of people switched. "The inversion of the cycle," Livi-Bacci continues, "[…] took place in the last third of the century, as Europe experienced a net migratory gain of 8 million in 1970–90 and another 27 million during 1990–2010." Loss became increase; the journeys were taken in the opposite way.

For the United Kingdom, according to the Office of National Statistics, net migration in 1975 was around *minus* 40,000. But for 2015 it had risen to *plus* 336,000. Imitating the broader European pattern, the direction of voyage is reversed. The European Union as a whole, by 2010, included 25 million immigrants who had arrived over the previous few decades from outside Europe: approximately 5 percent of the population. In the United States matters are harder to decipher. This is because Washington retains no record of emigration so the exactness of population movement, gains vs. losses, cannot be established. But the Department of Homeland Security estimated that in 2013 there were 13.1 million individuals with the status of Legal Permanent Resident (i.e., legally resident migrants).

Some 11.3 million illegal immigrants were believed to be present in the United States in 2014 though by definition that figure is impossible to confirm. The total population of the United States in 2014 numbered 318.9 million, with a legal and estimated illegal population of migrants therefore comprising something in the region of 7.65 percent of the whole.

The challenge for modern thinkers is to assess the implications of this. And it is also to be able to find ways of so doing. Horrified by the unforgotten memory of the Second World War, liberal Europe—its institutions, intellectuals, and politicians—has struggled to open debates about migration without invoking accusations of racism and recollections of the Final Solution. The liberal, humane argument, in turn, born from the un-faded recollection of the War and its gas chambers, has settled on a position that can rarely now brook inquiry. That position assumes a version of human universalism: that all cultures, the diversity of all ways of life, are equally acceptable and to be affirmed (again, at times, this requires the recovery of "non-judgmental" attitudes as a good). Multiculturalism—a word first recorded in English in 1957—will, in turn, succeed, the post-War argument says, because it is an expression of, and a faith in, that universalism. Multiculturalism assumes, though usually implicitly, that because each culture is equally entitled to respect or at least to be free from judgment, a plurality of cultures can coexist harmoniously in the same hosted space while retaining their own identities. This concept of mutual-harmony-with-identity is sometimes joined in the minds of the most extreme liberal intellectuals with bolder arguments that "national" and "cultural identity" are myths, forms of false consciousness, or divisive ideological tools. In addition, there have been cognate claims about "postnationality," a theoretical conception of human beings cooperatively existing without any specific sense of identity shaped by place (except perhaps the immediately local) or time. In the liberal consensus and in mainstream political debate the assumptions of multiculturalism and the certainty of its success have become well established. Diversity as an ambition has been accepted as a more-or-less unquestionable good.

Without a safe cultural and intellectual location for ongoing watchfulness about the meaning, implications, and achievability of diversity, however, the liberal West has, in turn, inadvertently created an opportunity for the establishment of exactly the same values from which it was turning. Liberal intellectuals and politicians have made interrogating the principles of diversity a form of moral (and even sometimes of criminal) infraction. And so, limiting possibilities for analysis, they have permitted, apart from anything else, the festering of bitterness and anger. The extreme Right has taken the occasion to exploit those feelings and present not an argument but an alternative: the revival of intolerance and, in some cases, literally of fascism. On the matter of migration, such politics has at times involved, and continues to involve, the direct affirmation of Nazi ideology recast in versions of White Supremacy. In their public visibility, members of the extreme Right have obtained both media prominence and electoral success—consider, for instance, Great Britain, France, The Netherlands, Switzerland, North America, Austria, or Hungary.

In the British Referendum on "Brexit" on June 23, 2016, which saw nearly a 52 percent majority voting in favor of leaving the European Union, there were many arguments made on Brexit's side. These included economic and national (as distinct from nationalist) justifications as well as a principled resistance to the idea of the European Union as a political project destined in due course, it was asserted, to founder. But a number of Brexit's supporters held extreme views on race. Notable after the announcement of the result was the rise in violent crime against, or verbal abuse of, European workers in (mostly) England, particularly of Poles. The genetics of the pro-Brexit result are complex and they include the profound frustration felt by many of those left behind by neoliberalism: those who have not profited from the wealth modern corporations and financial services have created. But distasteful views on race have flourished (if that is quite the word) alongside economic vexation, and they have done so in part because mainstream liberal politicians and liberal intellectuals have prohibited immigration and diversity to be discussed except in terms that must conclude in set ways. Those conclusions could be justifiable and describe the best that is achievable. But it is hard to be when it is too risky to explore them.

The arguments of those campaigning in the United Kingdom to "Remain" embraced as many diverse views as those on the opposite side. There were economic, cultural, and security anxieties about separation, a worry about the break-up of British Union, and optimistic or idealistic faith in the political and moral project of the EU itself. But there were extreme views on this side too (even if they are not often described as such). Championed in certain quarters of the debate, including by some pro-Remain intellectuals, was the ultra-liberal argument that open borders must be regarded only as a humane welcoming of men, women, and children in distress, and in no other terms: neither economic nor cultural, nor in terms of potential consequences to security, nor in relation to possible changes in the nature of rural, urban, or suburban life. This argument viewed any such considerations as morally reprehensible. Holders of these extreme liberal views on the Remain side, accordingly, were unable to negotiate with the worries of their opponents on the other extreme, or of anyone who hoped to investigate the implications of the extreme liberal argument, because opponents, or merely those asking questions, were always deemed beyond the pale. The level of debate was, at times, astonishingly low. The extremes on both sides possessed almost no common language with which to address each other, and no appetite to do so. Brexit exposed assumptions that have defined more general arguments about diversity and migration in the United Kingdom for decades even if they were not always directly relevant to the local and specific question of membership of the European Union in the summer of 2016. And in those general arguments is a general truth. Caught between the contemporary high liberal affirmation of diversity as an unquestionable good and the Far Right's assertion that foreigners are a source of national weakness, migration, cultural change, and cultural identity through time have become peculiarly hard to talk about without conflict or reproach.

A crude way of expressing one of the problems would be this. Non-Western cultures, in the most committed and intense of the liberal arguments, have traditions of which there is a moral imperative for liberal societies to respect. Forgetting the cultural histories of migrants arriving from beyond the borders of a liberal state, ignoring their ethnic identities and traditions, is unacceptable, and any criticism is comprehensible only as species of racism. But so, in the extreme cases, is an attempt to assess what impact open borders might have on the hosts themselves. Can questions about what home looks like be asked under such conditions? Certainly, liberal hosts have yet satisfactorily to articulate, without extremism or the accusation of extremism, the value, significance, and nature of their own localized pasts (whether "own" is defined by the obviously contingent category of a nation state or by something subtler and more demanding) and how those pasts might relate to an idea of belonging not only in space but also in time. Western hosts have yet seriously to consider, or properly allow themselves to consider, how such pasts relate or do not relate to a collective, if evolving, identity.

There is migration of another kind, too, which functions in a different way to challenge the modern individual's sense of the potential specialness of location and its traditions, histories, and cultures. It is

a truism to say that free-market capitalism claims to promote difference and choice and in fact has peculiarly promoted homogenization.
A truism that is—true. Such capitalism has sponsored not so much
the flourishing of individual enterprise, as it theoretically should, but
the expansion of monopolies and global giants, which are on first
glance the opposite of the free market's intention. In turn, the globalized market has generated, inevitably, the spread of uniformity—
as well as its energetic resistance from feisty independent producers
and businesses—across the towns and cities of the world. It might be
Mcdonald's that springs first to mind for many of us as a major early
player in this great march of global brands (the company opened in
1940 as a barbecue outlet, turning to burgers 8 years later). Whatever
else you can find when visiting a new city—Berlin, Chicago, Moscow,
Singapore—you can usually find a Big Mac and fries. (Of the 196
countries in the world today, those fries are for sale in 119 of them.)
But this near ubiquity is now true of a multiplicity of products and
commercial enterprises across the planet, from coffee shops to opti-
cians, from apartment hotels to beer. Anyone who visits a modern
city is likely to comprehend that replication is the new visitor experience; that urban centers are exchangeable to a point, consistent in
their un-strangeness.

   This outcome of globalization has compounded an awareness of
spatial intimacies jeopardized or connections with places lost. What
can it mean to have a relationship with a location that has mutated
into a version of many others? The recent history of shopping malls
and city centers can be substituted for the recent history of other
shopping malls and city centers from Dallas to Dubai. History understood as something distinctive to an environment—architectural, cultural, political, commercial—is hard conceptually and imaginatively
to access behind the same store fronts, the identical brand names, the
same globalized food and fashion chains. The conception of place,

an idea of a locality with a distinctive appearance, a distinctive set of customs, and a distinctive history, is problematized. We are invited by global capitalism to say, paradoxically, either that we feel at home anywhere (visiting the same restaurant in different continents) or that we feel at home nowhere because nothing is substantially different. Familiarity is not comforting only.

Modernity's rejection of serious attention to the study of the past, its reluctance even to compile the *Gedenkschrift* for history, has been my subject for most of this book. It is losing the past in general that has been my topic. But it is hard not to wonder what this blankness does to us when considering the more local issue of the relationship between history and place. Modernity's rejection of much of the past together with a commercial aspiration to establish imperialized brands, which has obscured the identity—visual, cultural, local, national—of urban sites, is joined with a deep Western unease about the relationship between what we know of pasts and what belonging could feel like. We have stopped ourselves from asking too much about that relationship, making it both politically and ethically injurious to do so. We have provided ourselves often enough with only the most impoverished of answers as a consequence. The near abolition in the Western world of an attentiveness to the rewards and achievements of history—generated by all the forces I have described in the preceding pages—does remarkably varied work in reducing our comprehension of who we are.

Early twentieth-century Futurism put modernity's rejection of history in aggressive form, considering the emblematic uselessness of a museum. "Museums: cemeteries!" declared Marinetti in 1909, who had wanted to demolish Venice and build a new city in concrete over the re-exposed mudflats: "[...] Museums: public dormitories where one lies forever beside hated or unknown beings. Museums: absurd abattoirs of painters and sculptors ferociously slaughtering each other with color-blows and line-blows, the length of the fought-over walls!" Only the future: if this is peculiarly the manifesto of pre–First World War Italian Futurism, it is not so inconsistent with the general and continuing Western commitment to tomorrow that determines our daily lives.

Karl Marx regarded an existence without history as a condition, and an indication, of the ideal society. Across all the topics of loss and mourning considered in this book, it seems to me that we do not have satisfactory ways to inquire, in almost any area of Western life, whether he was right or not. To our present state of ignorance about historical achievements we have not sufficiently raised— with Socratic persistence—the question of what living with such ignorance does to us. The struggle, the *attaque au fer*, against the multiple forms of elected forgetfulness, this slicing of our under-standing of history, is hard. But the Homeric effort is not worth giving up. The contest of memory with forgetfulness—which in its way is part of the contest of life with the grave—is essential, even as our own individual minds retain less and less through time, fading in recall like the vanishing of Thomas Hobbes's many particular Streets. With that which is more than personal memory—with col-lective recognition of what is worth remembering—is the precious chance of a richer experience of existence; an ampler, unsentimen-tal respect for the best achievements of men and women in the past; and a safer sense of our (temporarily) belonging in time and place amid a world that isn't ours.

Acknowledgments

My thanks first of all are to Haaris Naqvi at Bloomsbury in New York for his interest in, and helpful advice about, this book and to Stacey Glick, my agent in New York. Friends, family, and colleagues have given me ideas, sometimes without knowing, and I am grateful in particular to Kathie Adare, Tricia Ayrton, Dinah Birch, Nicholas Daly, David Fuller, Ben Hayes, Robert Hewison, Michael Hurley, Kevin Jackson, Elisabeth Jay, Margaret Kelleher, Clark Lawlor, Clare Morgan, Chris and Michelle O'Gorman, Clare Pettitt, David Pipe, Stephen and Rosslie Platten, Francis Pott, Louise Powell, Stephanie Rains, Simon Rennie, Corinne Saunders, Nicholas Shrimpton, Helen Small, Libby Tempest, Marion Thain, Andrew Thompson, Alice, Isobel, and Sam Williams, James Williams, and Jane Wright. I have been most grateful to John Bowen, Matthew Campbell, Valerie Cotter, Emily Cuming, Tony Crowley, Sally Gray, and Jay Prosser for friendship over the past few years, and especially to Graham Huggan and Sabine Schlüter, and to Kate Williams. I must thank the exceptionally helpful staff of the National Library of Scotland as I begin to make my home in Edinburgh and, at a very late stage in the completion of this book, the Minister and musicians of Canongate Kirk, on the Royal Mile. No one is responsible for the mistakes and (mis)judgments here, except me. *Forgetfulness* is for my parents, John and Joyce O'Gorman, with my love.

Edinburgh

References

In order not to interrupt the main text, there are no note cues. References for direct quotations, however, are as below. Note that where I am citing a book edition that is different from the first edition, I include the date of original publication in square brackets at the beginning of the parenthetical information detailing place of publication, publisher, and date. All citations from Shakespeare in the main text are to *The Oxford Shakespeare: The Complete Works*, 2nd ed., edited by Stanley Wells and Gary Taylor (Oxford: Oxford University Press, 2005); those to the Bible are to the King James Version in the 1769 Oxford "Authorized" edition. All references to the *Oxford English Dictionary* (*OED*) are to the electronic edition, available at www.oed.org. Where Kindle editions have been cited that do not have page numbers, I have simply indicated this: the reference can be traced using Kindle search functions. Translations, unless stated otherwise, are by me.

Prelims

Page vii—*Today the air ... sense*: Wallace Stevens, *Selected Poems*, edited by John N. Serio (New York: Knopf, 2011), p. 316.

Page vii—*We must not think ... one*: Walter Bagehot, *Lombard Street: A Description of the Money Market* (London: Dutton, 1910), p. 20.

Introduction

Page 1—*Here is a good deal … ruin*: Edmund Burke, *Observations on a Late Publication, Intituled "The Present State of the Nation"* (1769) from *The Works of the Right Honorable Edmund Burke*, 12 vols. (London: Nimmo, 1887), i.259.

Page 6—*CLOV: … always that*: Samuel Beckett, *Endgame*, most easily accessible from http://samuel-beckett.net/endgame.html.

Page 7—*Our loneliness … eschatology*: Peter Porter, "The Historians Call up Pain," most easily accessible from the digital edition of Porter's works, http://www. poetrylibrary.edu.au/poems-book/collected-poems-volume-i- 1961-1981-0287000.

Chapter 1

Page 17—*You do stir up … things*: Aeschylus, *Persai*, ll. 988–9, translated by Alan H. Sommerstein, Loeb Classical Library (Harvard: Harvard University Press, 2009), p. 123.

Page 20—*No man called Homer … long ago*: Adam Nicolson, *The Mighty Dead: Why Homer Matters* (London: Collins, 2014), p. 50.

Page 25—*Let us not forget … suppression*: Sigmund Freud, *Civilization and Its Discontents* in *The Standard Edition of the Complete Psychological Works of Sigmund Freud*, general editor James Strachey in collaboration with Anna Freud, assisted by Alix Strachey and Alan Tyson, 24 vols. (London: Hogarth, 1956–74), xxi.115.

Page 27—*hos cape fatorum … ignem*: Vergil, *The Aeneid*, translated by H. Rushton Fairclough, 2 vols., Loeb Classical Library (Cambridge, MA: Harvard University Press, 1916), ii.294–7 (p. 336).

Page 27—*Take them … undying fire*: Ibid., p. 337.

Page 30—*The glorious city of God … peace*: St. Augustine of Hippo, *The City of God* from *The Works of Aurelius Augustine, Bishop of Hippo*, translated by Marcus Dods, 15 vols. (Edinburgh: T&T Clark, 1871–6), i.1.

Page 31—*If Homer had remained … have had!*: Quoted in Ronald Gray, *Goethe: A Critical Introduction* (Cambridge: Cambridge University Press, 1967), pp. 203–4.

Chapter 2

Page 33—*Everybody in the crowded street ... appointment*: Virginia Woolf, *The Years* (London: Grafton, 1977), pp. 6–7.

Page 35—*It is difficult ... utterly new*: Benedict Anderson, "Memory and Forgetting" in *Imagined Communities: Reflections on the Origin and Spread of Nationalism* ([1983] London: Verso, 1991), p. 193.

Page 37—*Mr. Moore loved ... them*: Currer Bell [Charlotte Brontë], *Shirley: A Tale* (New York: Harper, 1850), p. 30.

Page 47—*honorable advancement in life*: Samuel Smiles, *Self-Help: With Illustrations of Character and Conduct* (London: Murray, 1859), p. 216.

Page 49—*great achievement ... worthless make-shifts*: William Morris, *News from Nowhere: Or, An Epoch of Rest, Being Some Chapters from a Utopian Romance* (Kelmscott: Kelmscott Press, 1893), p. 137.

Page 52—*All else for which ... their adoration*: *The Seven Lamps of Architecture* from *The Library Edition of the Complete Works of John Ruskin*, edited by E. T. Cook and Alexander Wedderburn, 39 vols. (London: Allen, 1903–12), viii.53.

Page 53—*There is no such thing ... forever*: Thomas De Quincey, *Confessions of an English Opium Eater*, 2nd ed. (London: Taylor and Hessey, 1822), p. 161.

Page 53—*[There] are but two ... reality*: *The Seven Lamps of Architecture* from *The Library Edition of the Complete Works of John Ruskin*, viii.224.

Page 54—*great Concourse ... just*: "Of Kings' Treasuries" from *Sesame and Lilies* (published 1865 but delivered in 1864), *The Library Edition of the Complete Works of John Ruskin*, xviii.80.

Page 55—*marvelously ... circumstance*: John Kenneth Galbraith, *The Affluent Society*, rev. ed. ([1958] London: Penguin, 1999), p. 50.

Page 55—*to praise revolutions ... present*: Herbert Butterfield, *The Whig Interpretation of History* (London: Bell, 1931), p. v.

Page 60—*who found for themselves ... oblivion*: George Eliot, *Middlemarch: A Study of Provincial Life*, 2 vols. (London: Blackwood, 1871–2), i.vi.

Page 63—*O but Tom ... beginning!*: George Eliot, *The Mill on the Floss*, 3 vols. (London: Blackwood, 1859), ii.89.

Chapter 3

Page 65—*Yesterday, Today ... Tomorrow*: "Yesterday, Today, Tomorrow," Leroy Altman, *Poem Collection: Shadows and Whispers* (Lulu.com, 2014), unpaginated.

Page 66—*moved on in scorching ... all things*: Benjamin Jowett (trans.), *The Dialogues of Plato, Translated into English*, 5 vols. (Oxford: Clarendon, 1892), i.165.

Page 67—*Everything had changed ... abstract*: Virginia Woolf, "Flying Over London", *Collected Essays*, 6 vols. (London: Hogarth, 1967), iv.171–2.

Page 68—*Wherever he happens ... another*: Washington Irving, "Rural Life in England," *The Sketch-Book of Geoffrey Crayon, Gent*, edited by Susan Manning (Oxford: Oxford University Press, 1996), p. 59.

Page 69—*The bourgeoisie cannot ... production*: Karl Marx and Friedrich Engels, *Manifesto of the Communist Party*, authorized English translation edited by Friedrich Engels (New York: New York Labor News, 1908), p. 12.

Page 69—*We stand on the last ... speed*: F. T. Marinetti, "The Founding and Manifesto of Futurism," in *Documents of 20th-Century Art: Futurist Manifestos*, edited by Umbro Apollonio, and translated by Robert Brain, R. W. Flint, J. C. Higgitt, and Caroline Tisdall (New York: Viking, 1973), pp. 19–24 (p. 20).

Page 71—*Researchers in the new field ... one of them*: Pico Iyer, *The Art of Stillness: Adventures in Going Nowhere* (New York: Simon & Schuster, 2014), p. 31.

Page 72—*Verily ... all things stream*: Lucretius, *On the Nature of Things: A Metrical Translation* by William Ellery Leonard (London: J. M. Dent, 1916), p. 198.

Page 73—*the enduring project ... expected*: Adam Phillips, *Missing Out: In Praise of the Unlived Life* ([2012] London: Penguin, 2013), p. xiv.

Page 75—*[Remember] that your business plan ... row*: Vaughan Evans, *The FT Essential Guide to Writing a Business Plan: How to Win Backing to Start Up or Grow Your Business*, 2nd ed. (Harlow: Pearson Education, 2016), p. xix.

Page 75—*is a handbook ... enterprises*: Front cover blurb for Alexander Osterwalder and Yves Pigneur, *Business Model Generation* (New Jersey: Wiley, 2010).

Page 75—*so yes ... our bones*: Olivia Laing, *To the River: A Journey Beneath the Surface* (Edinburgh: Canongate, 2011), p. 134.

Page 77—*is a way to pretend ... unknown*: Rebecca Solnit, *A Field Guide to Getting Lost* (Edinburgh: Canongate, 2005), p. 163.

Page 79—*Son of Tydeus ... Agamemnon*: Homer, *Iliad, Books 1–12* (Book 9), translated by A. T. Murray, revised by William F. Wyatt, Loeb Classical Library (Cambridge MA: Harvard University Press, 1999), p. 399, ll.53–4, 60–63.

Page 87—*Bold lover ... the goal*: John Keats, *The Complete Poems*, edited by John Barnard, 3rd ed. (London: Penguin, 1988), p. 309.

Page 89—*How could it be ... between them?*: Darian Leader, *What Is Madness?* ([2011] London: Penguin, 2012), p. 2.

Page 90—*But certainly for the present age ... profane*: Guy Debord, *Society of the Spectacle* (Bread and Circuses Publishing, 1977), Chapter 1, quoting Ludwig Feuerbach, *The Essence of Christianity*, 2nd German edition, translated by Marian Evans (George Eliot) (London: Chapman, 1854), p. xi. The full passage is: "But certainly for the present age, which prefers the sign to the thing signified, the copy to the original, fancy to reality, the appearance to the essence, this change, inasmuch as it does away with illusion, is an absolute annihilation, or at least a reckless profanation; for in these days illusion only is sacred, truth profane."

Page 92—*Despite all its rhetoric ... the new*: Mark Fisher, *Ghosts of My Life: Writings on Depression, Hauntology and Lost Futures* (Alresford: Zero Books, 2014), p. 14.

Page 93—*When an individual ... possible*: Robert Hewison, *Cultural Capital: The Rise and Fall of Creative Britain* (London: Verso, 2014), p. 7.

Page 97—*I have come ... antipodes*: Marguerite Yourcenar, *Memoirs of Hadrian*, translated by Grace Frick ([1951] London: Penguin, 1986), p. 31.

Chapter 4

Page 99—*I don't know ... forget it*: *Dostoevsky's Occasional Writings*, edited and translated by David Magarshack (Evanston, IL: Northwestern University Press, 1997), p. 317.

Page 100—*unwanted conduct related ... individual*: From p. 10 of the Equality Act (2010), Chapter 5, available on http://www.legislation.gov.uk/ukpga/2010/15/pdfs/ukpga_20100015_en.pdf, last accessed March 7, 2016.

Page 100—*We believe ... in the world*: From http://www.helpage.org/who-we-are/our-values-and-ambitions/, last accessed March 7, 2016.

Page 107—*Loneliness is a massive ... company*: From http://www.ageuk.org.uk/
health-wellbeing/relationships-and-family/befriending-services-
combating-loneliness/, last accessed March 7, 2016.

Page 101—*No matter how ... 'Ages of Man'*: Douwe Draaisma, *The Nostalgia
Factory: Memory, Time and Ageing*, translated by Liz Waters (New
Haven: Yale University Press, 2008), pp. 8–9.

Page 105—*Memory concerns ... alone*: From http://www.alzfdn.org/, last
accessed March 7, 2016.

Page 105—*It is estimated ... disease*: From http://www.alzfdn.org/
AboutAlzheimers/statistics.html, last accessed March 7, 2016.

Page 106—*a rare insight ... lives*: Advertising blurb from the back cover
of Christine Zimmerman, *Beyond Forgetting* (Create Space
Independent Publishing Platform, 2014).

Page 107—*Every year ... seconds*: From "Key Statistics" of the Stroke Association
on https://www.stroke.org.uk/sites/default/files/stroke_statistics_
2015.pdf, p. 4, last accessed March 7, 2016.

Page 108—*About 795,000 Americans ... seconds*: From http://www.
strokeassociation.org/STROKEORG/ AboutStroke/Impact-of-
Stroke-Stroke-statistics_UCM_310728_Article.jsp#.Vt2Wfn2LT4Y,
last accessed March 7, 2016.

Page 110—*Mrs. B. ... name*: Oliver Sacks, *Awakenings* ([1973] London: Pan,
1982), p. 63.

Page 111—*At one end ... Jobs*: Temple Grandin and Richard Panek, *The Autistic
Brain: Exploring the Strength of a Different Kind of Mind* ([2013]
London: Rider, 2014), p. 16.

Page 112—*need to keep ... work*: Simon Baron-Cohen, *Autism and Asperger
Syndrome: The Facts* (Oxford: Oxford University Press, 2008), p. 48.

Page 113—*Most researchers ... rush*: Temple Grandin and Richard Panek, *The
Autistic Brain*, p. 72.

Page 115—*It would be nice ... prodigies*: See http://www.theguardian.com/
tv-and-radio/2016/mar/09/the-a-word-autism-funnier-than-this-tv-
drama, last accessed March 9, 2016.

Page 116—*therapeutic culture ... perspective*: Dana Becker, *One Nation under
Stress: The Trouble with Stress as an Idea* (New York: Oxford
University Press, 2013), p. 154.

Page 118—*projection onto another ... conflicts*: From http://www.apsa.org/
content/psychoanalytic-terms-concepts-defined, last accessed March
7, 2016.

Chapter 5

Page 123—*Repetition ... life again*: Søren Kierkegaard, *"Repetition" and "Philosophical Crumbs,"* translated by M. G. Piety ([1843] Oxford: Oxford University Press, 2009), p. 3.

Page 124—*a matter of sorrow ... men*:
Theodore Dalrymple, *Our Culture, What's Left of It: The Mandarins and the Masses* (Cheltenham: Monday Books, 2010), e-book, loc.591.

Page 125—*Every verbal signification ... rivers*: Emmanuel Levinas, *Humanism of the Other* (1972), translated by Nidra Poller (Chicago: University of Illinois Press, 2003), p. 11.

Page 127—*Author's empire ... oneself*: Barthes's essay is most easily accessed from http://www.ubu.com/aspen/aspen5and6/threeEssays. html#barthes, last accessed April 8, 2016.

Page 128—*Impossible to know ... in you*: Adam Phillips, "Talking Nonsense and Knowing When to Stop," *One Way and Another: New and Selected Essays* (London: Hamish Hamilton, 2013), p. 291.

Page 141—*with a desire for goodness ... good*: Xenophon, *Conversations of Socrates*, translated by Hugh Tredennick and Robin Waterfield, edited by Robin Waterfield (London: Penguin, 1990), p. 73.

Chapter 6

Page 145—*How is your doom ... war?*: Vergil, *Aeneid*, Book I, translated by John Dryden (New York: Collier, 1909), p. 83.

Page 145—*a returne to Confusion ... every man*: Thomas Hobbes, *Leviathan*, reprinted from the 1651 edition (Oxford: Clarendon, 1909), p. 150.

Page 146—*a great distance of time ... Streets*: Ibid., p. 14.

Page 148—*excavating a barrow ... joy*: Arthur Conan Doyle, *The Hound of the Baskervilles: Another Adventure of Sherlock Homes* (London: Newnes, 1902), p. 163.

Page 149—*We sometimes feel ... rain*: W. H. Hudson, *Hampshire Days* (London: Longmans, Green, 1903), pp. 51–2.

Page 149—*I traced the Circus ... Rome*: Thomas Hardy, *Poems of the Past and of the Present*, 2nd ed. ([1901] London: Harper, 1902), pp. 44–5.

Page 151—*[We] crave to know … came*: Alfred Watkins, *The Old Straight Track: Its Mounds, Beacons, Moats, Sites and Mark Stones* ([1925] London: Abacus, 1974), p. xix.

Page 151—*Walking … world*: Rebecca Solnit, *Wanderlust: A History of Walking* (London: Penguin, 2000), p. 29.

Page 152—*what this period means … territory*: Charlotte Higgins, *Under Another Sky: Journeys in Roman Britain* (London: Jonathan Cape, 2013), p. xx.

Page 153—*are the descendants of memory and power*: Adam Nicolson, *The Mighty Dead: Why Homer Matters* (London: William Collins, 2014), p. 49.

Page 154—*But if [Penelope] shall … device*: Homer, *Odyssey*, Book 2, translated by A. T. Murray and George F. Dimock, Loeb Classical Library (Cambridge, MA: Harvard University Press, 1919), p. 55.

Page 154—*The English landscape … possess*: W. G. Hoskins, *The Making of the English Landscape* ([1955] Wimborne Minster: Little Toller Books, 2014), e-book.

Page 155—*But most of England … time*: Ibid.

Page 155—*Woods, like water … humanity*: Roger Deakin, *Wildwood: A Journey through Trees* ([2007] London: Penguin, 2008), unpaginated front end papers.

Page 156—*Anyone who lives in a city … long*: Robert Macfarlane, *The Wild Places* (London: Granta, 2007), p. 6.

Page 157—*Like being married … homelessness*: Malachy Tallack, *Sixty Degrees North: Around the World in Search of Home* (Edinburgh: Polygon, 2015), p. 214.

Page 158—*In today's fast-paced urban world … now*: Francis Pryor, *Home: A Time Traveller's Tales from Britain's Prehistory* (London: Penguin, 2014), p. xv.

Page 159—*To stand in an immense starred night … carpet*: John Lewis-Stempel, *Meadowland: The Private Life of an English Field* (London: Doubleday, 2014), p. 261.

Page 159—*We have this treeless waste … richer*: Mike Cawthorne, *Wild Voices: Journeys through Time in the Scottish Highlands*, unpaginated e-book (Edinburgh: Birlinn, 2014).

mechanics and shopkeepers … long ago: Henry David Thoreau, *Walking*, most readily accessible from http://thoreau.eserver.org/walking1.html, last accessed September 6, 2016.

Page 160—*Wood cuts most easily ... urgency*: Philip Marsden, *Rising Ground: A Search for the Spirit of Place* (London: Granta, 2014), p. 174.

Page 161—*It was what they knew ... journeys*: Philip Marsden, *The Crossing Place: A Journey among the Armenians* (London: Collins, 1993), pp. xix–xx.

Page 161—*all the inherited fear of lost land*: Ibid., p. 242.

Page 162—*amounted to 7 million ... during 1990–2010*: Massimo Livi-Bacci, *A Short History of Migration*, translated by Carl Ipsen (2010: Cambridge: Polity, 2012), p. 60.

Europe will be ... recovered: Ibid., loc.505.

Page 168—*Museums: cemeteries! ... walls*: F. T. Marinetti, "The Founding and Manifesto of Futurism," in *Documents of 20th-Century Art: Futurist Manifestos*, edited by Umbro Apollonio, and translated by Robert Brain, R. W. Flint, J. C. Higgitt, and Caroline Tisdall (New York: Viking, 1973), pp. 19–24 (p. 21).

Index

Aeschylus 17, 19, 29
Altman, Leroy 65
Alzheimer's disease 104–7, 111
Anderson, Benedict 35
Armenia 160–1
Asperger's syndrome 112–13
assessment criteria 135–9
Auden, W. H. 140
autism 11, 110–15

Bagehot, Walter viii
Baron-Cohen, Simon 112–13
Barthes, Roland 127–9
Bayley, John 60, 105–6
Becker, Dana 116
Beckett, Samuel 6
Bismarck, Otto von 21, 102
Bonaparte, Napoleon 34, 80
"Brexit" 14, 164–6
Brontë, Charlotte 37–8
Budget (UK finance statement) 88, 103
Burke, Edmund 1
Butterfield, Herbert 55

Carlyle, Thomas 56
Cawthorne, Mike 159
Chang, Ha-Joon 81
Christ Church, Oxford 38
Cognitive Behavioral Therapy
    11, 115–18
Coleridge, Samuel Taylor 111–12

commuting 68–9
Conan Doyle, Sir Arthur 148
Constable, John 61–4
Cromwellians 9, 34–5
Cross, Gary 94

Dalrymple, Theodore 123–4
Darwin, Charles 118
Deakin, Roger 155–6
Debord, Guy 90–1
Declaration of Independence (US) 35
dementia 11, 104–7, 111, 115
department stores 45–6
De Quincey, Thomas 53
Derrida, Jacques 126
Dickens, Charles 57–9, 76
Dostoyevsky, Fyodor 99
Draaisma, Douwe 101–2

Eliot, George 60, 90
"empathy" 137–8
Engels, Friedrich 69
Equality Act 2010 (Great
        Britain) 99–100
etymology of "memory" 2
euphemisms for forgetting 1, 2
Euripides 29
Evans, Vaughan 75

"feedback" 137–8
Fernyhough, Charles 3

Feuerbach, Ludwig 90
Fisher, Mark 92, 96
French Revolution 9, 33–7, 38, 61
Freud, Sigmund 2, 3, 6, 24–5, 86–7,
    104, 118–20
    Civilization and Its
        Discontents 24–5
    theory of first memories 2–3

Galbraith, John Kenneth 55
Geoffrey of Monmouth 270–8
Gestalt counselling 115–16
Goethe, Johann Wolfgang von 31, 80
Grandin, Temple, and Panek, Richard
    111, 113
Great Western Schism 42

Hardy, Thomas 149–50
Harris, Alexandra 156–7
Hewison, Robert 93
Higgins, Charlotte 152–3
Hobbes, Thomas 145–7, 169
Homer 15, 19–21, 22–3, 25, 29, 31, 75,
    79, 142–3, 147, 149, 153–4, 169
Hoskins, W. G. 154–5
House of Atreus 17–23
Hudson, William Henry 149, 150
Hungarian revolution (1848–9) 37

identity politics 131–5
"interruption science" 71–2
Irving, Washington 68
Iyer, Pico 71–2

James, William 118
Jamie, Kathleen 159
jokes 84–6
Jowett, Benjamin 66

Kanner, Leo 110
Keats, John 87
Kermode, Sir Frank 138–9
Keynes, John Maynard 82
Kirkegaard, Søren 123
Kissinger, Henry 73

Laing, Olivia 75
Leader, Darian 89–90
Levinas, Emmanuel 125
Lewes, George Henry 64
Lewis-Stempel, John 158–9
Livi-Bacci, Massimo 162
London skyline 95

Macaulay, Lord 55
Macfarlane, Robert 156
Magnusson, Sally 107
Mallarmé, Stephane 127
Marinetti, Filipino Tommaso
    69–70, 168–9
Marr, Andrew 108
Marsden, Philip 160–1
Marx, Karl 69, 86, 90, 131, 169
McCrum, Robert 108
Mcdonald's (burger restaurant
    chain) 167
Microsoft 70
"modernity," definition of 44–6
Morris, William 48–50, 55, 56, 60, 94
Morse, Samuel 40
Murdoch, Iris 105–6
Mycenae, ancient 8, 13, 17–22, 62, 63,
    139, 158

National Student Survey (UK) 139
Newgrange, Co. Meath 148
Nicolson, Adam 20–1, 153

Ordnance Survey maps 152

Paris 33–6
"personal development plan" 10, 76–8,
    79, 136
Phillips, Adam 73, 128–9
Place de la Concorde 34–6
Plato 66, 140, 143
polis 8, 23–31, 33, 35, 36, 140, 142
Porter, Peter 7
poststructuralism 12, 124–30, 135
Price, Harry 21
Proust, Marcel 39